DOG DAYS

DOG DAYS

Joyce Stranger

Michael Joseph
LONDON

First published in Great Britain by
Michael Joseph Ltd
44 Bedford Square
London WC1B 3DP
1986

British Library Cataloguing in Publication Data

Stranger, Joyce
Dog days.
I. Title
828′.91408   PR6069.T68

ISBN 0 7181 2680 7

Typeset by Alacrity Phototypesetters,
Banwell Castle, Weston-super-Mare.
Printed and bound in Great Britain by Billings, Worcester

Dedicated to my three grandchildren, Ruaraidh, Rebecca and Jacob, who weren't born when my book was dedicated to Jonathon, Mairi and Morag

Illustrations

Chapter One

Dog days.

High days and holidays. Days to enjoy. The hot days of summer, when we are young and full of energy and life is so exciting we can never wait for tomorrow, for the next moment, which we know will be tremendous fun.

There is all the unmapped future; mountains to conquer and ambitions to achieve.

Most people lose that as they grow older but those of us who have dogs, and enjoy our dogs (not all dog owners do), never lose it at all.

Every day is a dog day.

Every day we wake and are greeted by our companion dogs. How can any of us explain how we feel at that first moment, in the early morning, when the animal we have chosen to share our lives is standing by the door, waiting for it to open, to renew the pleasure of our presence.

Such simple actions bring delight to them: putting on our walking shoes; picking up the lead; taking the dog's dinner bowl out of the cupboard.

It doesn't matter whether we are royalty or rogues; our dogs don't care. To them we are all-important. What we are doesn't matter. Who we are doesn't matter. Our dogs reward us with their loyalty, as Kipling said, whether we give them a kick in the ribs or a pat on the head.

Thursdays to me now are the best dog days of all, when there is dog club. Up to thirty dogs a night, of all breeds and no breed, full of excitement, ready to do anything but work for their owners at first, and then, after a few weeks, a miracle occurs, and the bounding out-of-hand dog comes in at heel, tail wagging, owner happy and confident beside the dog. Then I know all

9

over again that small satisfying thrill that comes when a pupil has learned a lesson well.

For those weeks with me the dog is as important to me as my dog; its success as necessary, as until the dog is trained to a reasonable degree it can be a danger to itself and its owner. Bringing a dog under control is far more rewarding than is at first apparent.

The trained dog can go anywhere with you, meet anyone, even giving pleasure by visiting old people in homes and children in hospitals.

There's nothing quite like it, except for the occasions when, training my Trials hopeful, she performs so well that I want to hug her.

I never know what is coming through the door. It may be a Miniature Pinscher, five inches high and four months old, full of worry and self-importance, hilariously shouting defiance with all his might at all those enormous dogs he finds inside the room.

It may be a stately Great Dane, coming in regally, looking around her, taking everything in, chary of offering her friendship until she knows me, and then always turning her head and waving her tail when she sees me at the start of future lessons.

Big dogs and little dogs; dogs of pedigree and dogs with none. They all have to be trained.

'My pup's so wild,' an owner says breathlessly, towed in behind a cavorting gleeful minx who can't wait to get through the door.

'Were you staid and sober when you were only six years old?' I ask. 'Twenty-four weeks ago, your bitch wasn't even there! Did you learn to drive in only a few short lessons? She's so much learning to do.'

'My dog won't come when he's called.'

'Have you taught him? How does he know what COME means? He doesn't speak human. He only speaks dog.'

'I don't really want to come to dog club,' a forlorn voice says on the phone. 'I don't want competition. I don't want to have to teach all the things they do at Cruft's. I just want to control my dog.'

So few people understand what competition is about; not even, at times, I suspect, the judges. The rules for tennis are the same, whether you play for fun at the local club, just out for exercise, or, if you practise hard and learn to make every stroke perfectly, you may end up at Wimbledon.

If you learn the ways of teaching your dog, and then train your dog, using those ways to control him, you may do it so well you end up at Cruft's. Yet some of the dogs that go to Cruft's are almost uncontrollable outside the ring because their owners have never realised that what we teach in club was never intended at first for competition; it is the rules by which we live with our dogs. It's not, 'If your dog sits crooked, he'll lose points in the ring when you go to a show,' but 'If your dog sits crooked, then *he* is boss, not you, and until you show him you are boss, he won't either sit straight *or* respect you.'

The dog that tows his owner as if that owner were a liner and he were a tug, is in command of the situation. The owner has fitted in with the dog. My dog has to fit in with *me*.

With many dogs that's far from easy.

I spent some years trying to break the code of dog training. I was sure there was a code. I had used it all my life, having invented it myself, basing it on the way the dog behaved.

It worked perfectly until I bought Janus, my Golden Retriever, in 1971. Up to then my dog days had been borrowed days after we married. (There were always dogs in my parents' home.) I had helped friends with dogs: fed them, walked them, advised their owners, begged or borrowed them, as, though I couldn't live without dogs, the rest of my family could. They didn't really fit into our way of life. I did have to admit that.

My family did allow me to have a Siamese cat! Kym, who was as much a handful as any dog, satisfied a little of my yearning. Not much, as I wanted a dog. I had never, until I married, lived without a dog, and my only hope was that one day I could say 'I'm getting a dog,' without having a violent argument. We nearly got divorced on the second day of our honeymoon when I met a litter of St Bernard puppies. I lost that argument – we did have a very small flat after all!

I so rarely seemed to do what I wanted; always what the family wanted, and life was passing me by. It was the eternal feminine wail, that has led to Women's Lib, but in those days there was no Women's Lib and I felt a freak.

I had to have some life of my own; had somehow to satisfy that craving for animals that has always dominated me; not to the point of spoiling them. I want them as animals, not substitute humans. I don't want their love because of a lack of family love. I have that in plenty, and am very lucky. I want them for their lack of knowledge of our human condition, to restore my sense of proportion, as you can't really worry yourself sick about an imminent nuclear holocaust when your dog is black determined to go out and you can walk off those feelings of depression as you watch the animal enjoy just being alive.

Something had to change, but I didn't know what. If I tried to say what I felt everyone just said 'Oh, don't be silly,' or made me a cup of tea and said I'd feel better tomorrow!

'Poor old Mum. She's off again!'

I stopped boating, which I hated, and escaped for my holidays to friends with dogs; helped socialise pups; helped train gundogs to accept the dummy bird; helped on farms where the dog was a major part of the farm life.

I lived in the suburbs, but I wrote every hour I could and lectured as well, until I had enough money to buy my own car, and then I was never at home after lunch. I was out in the country, living the life I wanted above all things, and getting more material for my books. I was riding and then helping with the horses; visiting farms, and standing with the great Shires nuzzling my hair; out watching the farmer train a young sheepdog; at a Sheepdog Trials; in kennels, watching a litter of pups find their legs; out in the fields, talking softly to a small startled foal, who wasn't at all sure he ought to trust a mere human. Holding the bottle for an eager orphan lamb, almost dragging the teat off, his small tail whizzing like a propellor.

I was at Belle Vue watching the Police Dog competitions; I was out in fields with police dogs; I was trying to ride a police horse, making sure all the articles I wrote were about farming

12

and animals, which was fine until the days of the NUJ and closed shops, when I had to think out my life all over again, as I am not eligible to join the NUJ. (I do belong to the Institute of Journalists, who have different criteria for membership.)

I lived in a constant state of envy, coveting not my neighbour's goods but all my friends' animals. I didn't want new carpets, three-piece suites or diamonds. I wanted a dog! Perhaps five or six dogs, and a few sheep and rabbits and ferrets and pheasants; a few cows and a donkey and a cat or three; but meanwhile I'd settle for just one dog of my own when Kym died.

Since I hadn't a dog and my dog-loathing Siamese was still alive I compensated. During my holidays I was in Ireland, with three Springer Spaniels and a black Labrador as my constant companions, borrowed from my host.

Helping feed the wild duck in an Irish version of Slimbridge, just starting up. The wild drakes flew to our buckets, before we could reach the pens, their wings thrashing our faces, their hungry beaks dipping into the grain. It was always a race to get to the pens before all the food went, with the drakes clinging to us, rather alarmingly fierce in their desperate bid for easy pickings.

I was out with my host sitting in a hide watching for pinemartens. We didn't see a flicker of fur for all our long cold wait, yet next day the farmer saw her with her young, within yards of where we'd been hiding. Was the wind wrong, bringing her wary nose news of the two hidden watchers? Did we stink of dog?

Up in a hide built in a tree at midnight, watching for badgers. Two boars fought beneath me, rolling and snarling, sounding like giant dogs. The victor left behind him a wounded animal, lying for a long time beneath my tree, sucking at his wounds and whimpering.

Out to visit a foxcub, and play with her (a little painfully) and watch her dancing like a kitten, playing with a feather. Fox cubs aren't in the least like puppies; they are mercuric creatures, much more like cats. There I met Bill Geldart who had come to draw her. He is as much animal orientated as I, and we were

13

both late home that day as we explored our animal interests. He has drawn my hardback fiction book covers for both Dent and Michael Joseph ever since. The little foxcub we both met that day is on the cover of *Never Tell a Secret* and has her place in the story. The cat on that cover is my own Chia, then a youngster, now an elderly and sometimes grumpy matron of fourteen.

Bill enjoyed putting my animals on his covers. Puma, my German Shepherd who died in 1981, is on the cover of *Paddy Joe at Deep Hollow Farm*, together with a pony Thomas, who Bill met, and whose owner wrote me a letter containing his story.

We've had some hilarious expeditions, looking for animals to draw for the various covers. When we wanted Siamese kittens for him to draw for *Kym*, we visited a house full of kittens, exploding from the furniture, using us as trees, flying up the curtains, diving up Bill's trouser leg!

Later we visited a small house whose owner rescued cats. There were cats all over the garden and all over the house; there was an indescribable stink and the most peculiar and unpleasant things lurked in odd corners! We politely refused a cup of tea.

Those days were yet to come. That was a long way into my unknown future.

I continued writing about animals I had met and spent time with. Borrowing animals, trying to fulfil a need that is impossible to explain to those who couldn't care less if there are animals or not, was totally unsatisfying.

Life was flying past at a terrifying rate. The family were suddenly grown up. The twins were both at college. Nick was in Glasgow studying to be a vet. Anne was in Sheffield reading Zoology. Andrew had started a sandwich course in electronics, but got fed up with college when students kept going on strike and left to start his work, and study at evening classes. He was either out or working in his bed-sitting room.

Kenneth was a very busy executive, who came home at night and barely heard me if I spoke, and then went off on exotic trips around the world, coming back exhausted, with indigestion and jetlag.

14

I seemed superfluous to everybody's lives; useful to do the washing and shopping and get the meals, of course. I listened to everybody and doled out sympathy which was often needed; for broken hearts and heartburn of a different kind. Nobody ever listened to me. Nobody even knew what I did with my spare time; they just didn't seem interested.

Occasionally, perhaps two or three times a year, I might have the vast excitement of a firm's dinner. I sat in the overheated rooms and ate the food and thought of a fresh wind blowing over green fields, and of running water, and the ducks in Ireland, and I felt stifled. People seemed to know one another and gossiped, talked about family, or about yoga and Weightwatchers. I wondered if the badgers still fought at Garnafailagh, and one evening, not being able to take part in any conversation, I had an idea for a book and almost wrote the first chapter of *The Honeywell Badger*.

'What on earth were you thinking about?' Kenneth asked on our way home.

'Badgers,' I said. He didn't answer. He had probably long ago concluded his wife wasn't normal!

We were both deprived as his longing was for a tall ship and a star to steer her by; he had a small ship and brief holidays and a wife who was seasick. I often wonder how we managed to stay together for forty years; this year I was given forty heathers for my Ruby wedding present.

It seems like for ever, yet it's very difficult to believe we are supposed to be old, as I race with my dog, maybe not at the speed I used to but far faster than my contemporaries who are dogless. Chita trots beside me, eager to see what is going to happen next.

Usually I sat at home and had an egg for supper, with Kym helping me, while Kenneth took VIP visitors out for meals, and then came home and recounted the menu. I doubt if he knew how often he nearly had my books chucked at him!

I was daunted one day when he asked if I would entertain a VIP's wife as no one else was free. My life was hardly the kind she would want to share. I bought a new outfit and made a list of

15

places we could visit: the art gallery; a concert; a couple of stately homes.

I went to pick her up at her hotel and we sat over coffee and discussed where we should go. She seemed about as enthusiastic about my suggestions as I was.

'Look,' I said in despair. 'Normally I'd be at the Kennels. They breed German Shepherds. Would you like to come?'

She came to life, and raced off and changed into slacks; we called in at home for me to get out of my best-occasion clothes and into familiar tatty kennel gear, and spent a heavenly day playing with puppies.

'It's the nicest entertainment I've had,' she said happily when we met the two men. I wasn't sure what they thought of it and my best beloved told me quite plainly I must have been mad. She would have hated it. He hadn't seen her with those puppies.

Then Kym died.

I had had enough of loneliness. Now I would buy my own dog. I bought him in too much of a hurry, not asking the right questions. If I'd known what I know now I wouldn't have bought him at all.

And I would have missed a whole exciting new way of life.

Chapter Two

I knew I had a good grounding for rearing the Golden Retriever pup I had bought. I had been with dogs of all sorts and all breeds. I'd walked them, helped train them, helped nurse them; had driven them and their owners to the vet (as few wives had cars of their own in those days). I was in high demand. None of those dogs was in the least difficult to teach. Nor were any of our family dogs; some we had for many years, some only briefly. There were Ricky and Thor, the fighting Bull Terrier; my constant companion for fifteen years, Turk, an Airedale cross who was more Airedale than anything else; and Paddy the little Sealyham cross.

I'd studied animal behaviour and dog psychology. I'd studied the behaviour of wild dogs, though that was by proxy as I'd read every book I could find on the subject, including Farley Mowat's classic *Never Cry Wolf*.

It should help me understand any dog, I thought. Dogs couldn't ever be that different.

Janus was.

My methods didn't work for this pup. He seemed half crazy. Lovable, but potty. He didn't hear my voice; he never listened. He blundered through the world clumsily and out of control.

Something had to be wrong.

So I went to club.

It was the start of a long pilgrimage, looking for people with real knowledge, not people who had bought an easy dog, gone into competition, done a lot of winning because they had a particularly clever dog, and, with experience of only one dog, set out to teach others.

My teachers had Collies or German Shepherds.

They didn't have Golden Retrievers.

17

At the time I didn't realise that that was one clue in a long line of clues that led me to wonder about the way dog clubs are sometimes run.

'Don't clap your hands at him,' said an earnest Collie owner, whose Collie was a bundle of nerves. 'It will terrify him.' A noise-shy gundog? She had to be joking.

Noises never worried Janus; he could take the loudest noise and not even flinch. Also, retrievers are supposed to be gundogs. A gunshy retriever is a crime.

'It's you,' they said. 'You can't control a dog at all. You oughtn't to have a dog.'

They were the experts, weren't they? I hadn't started to ask questions then. I hadn't discovered that a lot of my so-called 'instructors' had come to club themselves only the year before and their experience with dogs was far less than mine. I hadn't realised that when they said 'I worked in kennels,' which sounds impressive, it had to be translated as 'I helped in kennels every Saturday when I was at school and washed the dogs' dishes,' or 'I worked for six weeks and didn't like cleaning up and left.'

I hadn't discovered either that breeding dogs could be a front for dealing in dogs; that having boarding kennels could mean operating an appalling slum; that having done Working Trials could mean you'd tried once ten years ago, made a mess of it and never done it again.

Oddly, I hadn't realised that other people don't always tell the truth. If I wasn't truthful at school we had to learn a psalm every day for a week; and if I wasn't at home, my mouth was washed out with soap. It made me dead honest, but when other people lie, they think the rest of the world lies too, so my truths weren't believed.

I hadn't realised that anyone can start a dog club, with no experience at all. I bought my dog trustingly, thinking everyone operates as I do; I was wrong. I went to club, trustingly, thinking these people really knew.

I wanted help. Janus pulled; he pulled me over several times. Traffic terrified him and he bolted if he saw a milk float; we took off at top speed, with no chance of me stopping.

18

I didn't believe it was me as for the past year I had been training a friend's Labrador as all the family worked. Oddly he was the reason that finally brought me to buying my own dog. He was the last straw. With the Labrador I had a part-time dog, a biddable dog, a dog that sat when told, that stayed when told, that came when called, that walked beside me for miles, never pulling at all.

Then came the day when, if I appeared, his owners were forgotten. I was more important to him. I taught him his manners so I was pack leader; they just fed him and gave him shelter. I gave him fun and the satisfaction of learning, using his brains, working with me as a partner.

I was the one he greeted with enthusiasm.

He sat in the window, waiting for me, till I came.

We were going out to the park to do all those interesting fun things, not just go for a boring walk. He was going to use his brains, not just his body. He never knew which game we would play next.

The come game?

That was lovely as he was able to greet me every time he came, excited to be with me again, but when the excitement spilled over and threatened to become out of hand, I said SIT, and he sat, head up, ears pricked, eyes bright, eager, wagging his tail.

'Aren't I a clever dog?'

People who don't train their dogs miss so much pleasure as the dog loves to be part of the family, earning his keep, not just a passenger, yelled at often for being in the wrong place at the wrong time, doing the wrong thing.

Soon he liked being with me so much that his owners weren't happy. I had become more important than they were, so I said goodbye to him for ever. It had to be that way. He was their dog.

After that I found the afternoons empty. No more walks, relaxing with an eager dog beside me, always ready for a game.

I rang friends: 'How about a game of tennis?'

'Sorry, I'm tied up.'

By now Kym was dying. He had cancer. It was only a matter of weeks; and then of days; and then he was gone. I was alone in the house. Kenneth had gone to Germany. The house was big and empty, and there was no one to greet me when I came home.

There was another publicity occasion, at a cat show, which seemed to be a bit batty, but I had no say. Going to London to sign books, leaving home at 6 a.m. No food available on the train in spite of announcements to the contrary, and a derailment in front of us. We were rerouted.

At one point I found myself sitting for nearly an hour contemplating some sewage works neatly tucked under a motorway flyover. I looked at my companions and said:

'The Ancients left us rose-red cities half as old as time; we leave concrete flyovers and sewage works.'

You don't speak on English trains and above all you don't come out with remarks like that. I had the feeling that if everybody could have changed carriages they would have done! We finished a remarkably boring journey in icy silence.

We arrived three hours late. I rushed through London in a taxi that had never heard of the venue, and was greeted by the sales manager with, 'I've a children's party. Here you are.' I was left with a friend who had nothing to do with the books, in a hall full of people who had come to see cats, not to buy books, which was reasonable enough at a cat show. I'd thought it a batty idea in the first place.

My friend found a ham sandwich for me; she had lunched while waiting for my train.

The ham was green. The coffee that came with it was indescribable.

Only three people bought books. I'd had to pay my own train fare. This was supposed to be a publicity occasion and I should have been grateful. I also had to sell my own books, so I felt like the hired help again.

I left the books and wandered round looking at the gorgeous cats, which was the only bright spot in a remarkably horrible day.

My friend left, promising to order a cab to come for me and get me to my train. The cab driver had to pay £1.50 to get in, and find me, as nobody knew where I was or who I was. He swore at me because of it. I had twenty books left. What did I do? I left them to the cat show. I no longer cared.

They weren't pleased, but how could I carry them back on the train?

The cab driver continued to swear as I climbed into the cab and I burst into tears. It stopped him in his tracks. He had the money repaid to him. I recovered and he began to ask questions. I hadn't eaten since 5 a.m. I'd had a lousy day, and had only sold three books. I felt neglected and rejected.

'You need a union, mate,' he said. 'They shouldn't do that to a dog!' I was inclined to agree.

When we reached Euston he put me on the train, and asked the dining car people, who were cooking their own meal, if I could have a sandwich and a cup of tea.

'She can b---- well wait,' was the reply.

I sat, smelling sausages, not much caring whether I got home or not. I felt much better after I'd eaten.

Sitting in my empty house, thinking of that occasion and others not much better, I suddenly thought I was an absolute fool. It didn't sell books; it didn't do me any good. If I had a dog I would be tied. I couldn't go on any more ghastly train journeys and be treated as if I had no rights at all, but was only there as a paid entertainer. I wasn't an entertainer and I'd never yet had a fee that met my expenses, let alone paid for my time.

Things are different now, and all my visits in the last three years have been rewarded with a reasonable fee and full expenses. One couldn't operate any other way; it's no longer 30p a gallon for petrol.

This was 1971.

I bought my dog.

Now I had my dog. I had never seen such a potty pup. He didn't behave in the least like any of the dogs I'd known before, and I'd known a lot of dogs. He was exceptionally affectionate which made it impossible to do what the vet suggested and return him to the breeder. After a few days both the vet and I were positive he was older than we had been told (13 weeks old)

21

and had already been returned at least once, if not more often.

From over twelve years experience of frequent Golden Retriever pups coming to club, I'd say he was at least five months old when I bought him. This was confirmed by one of the few good instructors I met in his early days. There were only two, one at each of the first two clubs I joined. But still neither of them could account for my dog. Both were sure it was me.

Something had to be wrong, but it just wasn't possible to put one's finger on the exact trouble. He was very unusual. A most peculiar dog, in so many ways. He never, ever, listened. He looked at us; he stared at us; he watched our faces, if he felt like it.

He would obey me always if I used my hands on his body, making him perform the action I wanted. He didn't seem able to learn it; although I said the right words over and over, they made no impression at all.

He seemed incapable of learning, though he did know all about food. He was always extremely hungry, which wasn't surprising as food knew little about him, and was apt to come out an hour after eating as a liquid stream.

In those early days I wasn't going to confess to anyone, not even my very supportive vet, that I was beginning to wonder if I hadn't been an utter fool. I'd never known a dog like this. Maybe I wasn't fit to own a dog.

They showed me, in club, how to train him. Use your voice, they said. Janus didn't know about voices. He did know about signals. You can't do that; you must learn to find a voice that he does listen to, they said. Suppose he's off lead, at a distance, with his back to you?

I knew what happened then. I could bawl till my throat was sore. He didn't take any notice at all.

I used signals at home; I tried to use my voice in club. Janus didn't want to know.

It took four years to discover he was deaf. Four years to realise it was not me, it was my dog; that all the advice in the world had been unhelpful, as nobody ever told me how to train *that* dog.

It's so easy to be smug when you own an easy dog. It's so easy to be smug when you can put the dog that won't fit into the house into kennels or sell it to someone else. It's so easy to be smug when you have never owned a real tearaway.

People forget that every single dog is different.

There are no rules.

I have evolved my own way of dealing with dogs at my club. It isn't the way I was taught; it isn't the way most clubs operate.

Who taught me?

My dogs taught me. My deaf Janus; and his German Shepherd companion Puma, bought in 1972, who had lead poisoning as a pup that affected her learning capacity, and, later, her eyes, and blinded her. I told their story in my book *Two's Company*.

Then, in 1977, came my wicked little minx, the worst puppy I have ever met, bar one, and he was her nephew. Now she is eight. She is the best canine companion I have ever had. She has provided material for three books already: *Three's a Pack*, *Two for Joy* and *A Dog in a Million*. She is part of this one too, still teaching me daily that dogs are never what you expect; that every dog is different, and that some dogs, but very few, are so full of life and energy that they are a hazard to themselves. Their speed endangers their lives, unless they are trained to a very high degree and controlled like police dogs.

In my club I try to study every individual dog and find out what makes *that* dog want to work. It's different with every one, as my three difficult dogs taught me. If I meet a problem I am lucky in having met a number of really qualified people who are at the end of my phone and will give advice, if they can.

Among them are Eric Roberts, who retaught me a few years ago and to whom I owe a great debt of knowledge and experience; and my friend Bini, who is a police sergeant in charge of choosing the dogs as well as training them, and has years of experience behind him. I stay with him and his wife when I go to Trials in their area.

But my dogs have taught me far more than any humans ever have about dogs.

23

If you want information, it is best to get it from the horse's mouth!

So my dog clubs are based on the ways I learned of training very difficult dogs indeed, and wild animals; not from anyone else, but from my own experiences; with a badger cub, and a couple of foxcubs; and then, with a hawk. They gave me knowledge of dealing with nervous dogs, of which there are far too many these days.

You have to be so careful when you buy.

Most pups are outgoing; but genuine nerves often seem to me only to appear at adolescence and a previously bold pup sometimes turns shy. A shy one may turn overbold! Animals don't read books, or think about rules laid down by humans who haven't met enough of them to learn that nothing is that easy!

We were laughing the other day at an indignant breeder of Labradors who had expected to get a litter of blacks and yellows according to Mendel. She had all blacks. But it just depends on what sperm meets which egg; there is no reason at all why they should divide according to rules that, so far as I know, were worked out on fruit flies that have millions of eggs.

Geneticists produce formulae. I don't believe dogs know about formulae. I once asked my vet how long a mare took to foal. 'I can't tell you exactly,' he replied, 'mares can't read.'

Dogs and bitches can't read either.

Mate black and white, they say, and you get one black and one white and two mixed; but nobody gets piebald black and yellow Labradors.

Nature isn't like that at all.

Many breeders do repeat matings because the first litter was good. Goodness knows why the second should be the same. My brother and two sisters and I are the result of repeat matings and we couldn't be more different!

I shall never forget Jim Gould, whose farm at Lymm, Wilderspool Hall gave me the material for two of my books. He was one of the best farmers I have ever met.

'There's just one thing predictable about animal life,' he said.

24

He turned to me, with a wicked little twinkle in his eye. 'It's always completely unpredictable. You never know what will happen next.'

He had rung to tell me to come over and see a little red and white calf that had just been born to one of the cows in his pedigree black and white herd. There was panic. What was wrong with the bull? There was a frantic investigation as he was being used for Artificial Insemination, and if he wasn't a pedigree ... wow! Research showed that the early imported Friesians, that came from Holland, could be either colour. This was a throwback. A throwback to many generations before. It can happen at any time.

Trouble is, people never stop to think!

Chapter Three

I soon discovered, with my dogs, that many dog club instructors don't teach you how to teach *your* dog. They either teach you how to teach *their* dog, which isn't much help as you don't own a dog like that, or they pass on a rule-of-rote set of exercises taught at one of the training courses.

These are fine, applied to certain dogs. They do not apply to *all* dogs. Some, the really sensible dogs, lie down quietly whenever they are not needed; others roam the house like lost spirits, needing someone to tell them what to do, as they need a pack leader. Nobody recognises this.

I have been on four courses and have four Instructor's Certificates. Not one of those courses ever emphasised the fact that all dogs are different and on occasions you just have to use your wits and find a way, that is *not* cruel, of convincing the dog that he might as well lie down, as you are boss and he is not and he is going to do exactly as he is told, and not be a major nuisance all the time.

Janus was the sort of dog that adores a rough house; pull his ears, play hard and run into him, so that he could barge back, and his ears were up, his eyes were bright and his tail was wagging.

'This is fun. They're playing my kind of game. I understand that,' his laughing eyes said to me.

Pat him hard, race with him, and he trained fast once you used signals. Audrey Wickham, who is now married to Edward Hart who writes books on farming subjects, cracked one code for me with Janus, though even she didn't know why that method worked and no other.

Janus pulled. Nothing stopped him; you could jerk at his lead till he fell over. That was great, and the more you did it, the harder he pulled, as, enjoying that sort of rough game, he thought it was just part of the fun.

Audrey, who breeds the Sadghyl Collies which work very successfully in Obedience, came to club and saw me with Janus. No one knew what to do with him. They all knew it was me, and even though most of them didn't say so, I could read those scornful glances and rolled eyes as I tried to convey to my idiot dog that this kind of behaviour just wasn't on.

Their dogs didn't behave like that. Most of them had biddable bitches, most of those being Collies. It is so easy to be smug when you have an easy dog.

Owners of Golden Retrievers have to learn that these dogs are different; they are full of life and have a misplaced sense of humour. They are apt to test you to the limit, not by defiance, as other breeds may, but by sheer idiocy. Janus would lie on his back and bicycle with a paw in his mouth, looking at me sideways to see how I took this piece of nonsense.

I once judged an exemption show. These are little fun shows, not run according to normal Kennel Club rules, as you can enter unregistered dogs and cross breeds at them. It was lovely, as I didn't have a mixed class of all breeds. I had two Beginner classes, one of gundogs only; the other of German Shepherds (Alsatians: it's the same breed, which reverted to its pre-1914 war name a few years ago). I did enjoy my day. All those gorgeous dogs to watch.

It is so much easier to judge dogs of the same breed, when working, against one another; and not have to judge a mixture of breeds that move differently and work differently and aren't really comparable.

The owners of the Goldies came into the ring, all with the same expressions on their faces, as these were young inexperienced dogs.

'He's awful,' one man said in despair, as his big tough fellow towed him towards me, with that indescribable grin that only a Goldie can put on.

I laughed.

'I've lived with one for nearly ten years,' I said. 'He's

27

stubborn, he's headstrong, he's apparently unteachable and he's gorgeous!'

I knew all about living with a stubborn dominant Golden Retriever.

His owner relaxed and grinned, and they did a very good round.

In despair I asked Audrey if she'd help me. She was working in a boarding kennels, handling dogs all day. Other club instructors were only handling their own dogs. She had to be much more experienced. Also she had twelve Collies of her own as well as a German Shepherd and a Papillon, a game little fellow.

We went daily to the car park at the Wizard, at Alderley Edge. Janus was tied to my thigh by a crepe bandage. He couldn't pull. No commands were needed; I could pat his head. After six weeks of this he understood that when he was on the lead he walked beside me; he didn't race ahead and try to pull me over.

It makes sense now that I know he was deaf and couldn't hear any commands at all, so never associated words with the pulling.

He improved so much that Audrey decided that we would go to Carlisle and enter their dog show. I thought she was pushing me a bit, but we went together. She was competing in far higher classes than I. Janus and I were to start in the nursery stakes.

Carlisle is a lovely show. They have rosettes for ten places; sixty dogs compete in a class. To my delight we came home with an eighth place in the Beginner class, which is the lowest, a tenth place in the Novice class, which is next up, and won the Rupert Cup for the Golden Retriever with the highest percentage at the show, which was 96 per cent. Twelve years later I still have those two rosettes, which are three-tier, navy-blue and white and much cherished. Tangible memories of Janus. A friend looked at them, and said, 'No one can take those away from you.'

When I went back to club I was so excited I told the woman sitting next to me.

She stared at me in disbelief.

28

'Janus won a cup for best Golden Retriever? Oh, well, it will be something to remember him by,' she said, obviously sure it had been an absolute fluke.

Janus won over forty rosettes and two more cups before he retired, and the big Best Golden Retriever rosettes have pride of place on the wall. He tied first a number of times in Open and Championship shows, but we never won the runoff. We have a number of seconds.

I do owe that to Audrey and to no one else, as if she hadn't taken the trouble to help me it would have been a very different story. I can't repay her; I can try and pass on all that she and others as knowledgeable have taught me.

There are relatively few *really* knowledgeable people about these days in dogs. It's not like the old days when you served your apprenticeship in a well run kennels and learned through contact with people who had vast experience.

Today is the day of the instant expert. I don't feel all that knowledgeable but when I hear some of the incredible advice handed out to my club members by people who are new to dogs yet are breeding or competing with them, I do know that I have some experience. I never hand out advice on something I don't know; I ask the experts.

I find that the older you get and the more you learn, the more aware you are, if you are sensible and not conceited, of the vast amount of knowledge you don't have time to learn. All those breeds I have never met, like the Shar Pei. All those dogs I have never seen working. All those problem dogs that I receive letters about and try to help, but you really need to see the dog. The kind of advice you give by letter is only partly useful; if you actually watch the dog, you see what he is doing and may have seen that before, and know why.

Without seeing him, without knowing his full history, you are only guessing. I try to help by letter, but books and letters never make up for practical experience.

Some of the advice given to me has been absolutely absurd. I was told, by a number of people, to destroy Janus, as he had hip dysplasia and pancreas deficiency and wasn't fit. Neither disabled him; both were controlled. He lived to be thirteen years old.

I was told to destroy Puma, as the lead poisoning would have ruined her.

It did contribute to her early death, but I had Puma for nine years and wouldn't have missed her for the world. Her rosettes hang on the wall; over forty of those. I still have her record book full of prize cards, many of them Firsts.

I framed her Junior Warrant, for having twenty-five points gained at shows before she was eighteen months old. Three points for a First at a Championship Show, where a dog can be awarded a Championship Certificate, and one for a First at an Open Show. We had a cliffhanger situation with two weeks to her being eighteen months old and three points to gain. In fact she gained six in those weeks and had over the marks needed.

Three Championship Certificates under three different judges make a dog a Champion. Mind you, ninety judges might not award some Champions a certificate, but that's the way it goes. Puma won one Championship Certificate, at the National Working Breeds Show at Stoneleigh in 1977. That was a day to remember!

That too is framed and has pride of place on my study wall beside her photograph.

I was told to put Chita down as she was so wild and I'd never be able to train her. I gave up Obedience three years ago as I prefer Working Trials. That is far more of a challenge and much more difficult and better for my type of dog: active, eager, energetic, needing to use her brains.

Janus remained biddable; he had his moments, which I knew later were due to having his head turned away from me so that he couldn't see my signals. I recognised his odd expression when my friend Joy's old Sheltie began to go deaf. Pepper would look at us, knowing that we were doing something that ought to relate to him, with an intent expression of deep concentration, combined with puzzlement, on his face that I recognised at once.

That expression was what was so odd about Janus as a puppy.

He was trying desperately to understand something impossible. Though you may teach a deaf person about sound, you can never teach a deaf dog that others don't share his silent world. Humans have an advantage he can never have. That of comprehension. Nobody thought of a deaf pup.

You can't compete with a deaf dog, I was told, and once I knew he was deaf we had to withdraw. I suppose they thought that handlers may use cruel methods to teach the dog, but the signal methods aren't at all cruel. In fact my informants were wrong. Deaf dogs may not be shown in Breed, but they may work in Obedience and Trials. I learned that too late.

So Janus taught me a good deal that is denied to people who have easy dogs.

Puma was quite different.

She was a gentle biddable bitch, very anxious to please, who cringed if you raised your voice. Say 'Oh, Puma,' in a disapproving tone and she grovelled. 'Please, don't be cross. I didn't mean to do wrong. I didn't know.' You could almost hear the words from the attitude of misery she assumed.

You couldn't play the barging game with Puma. Puma's way of greeting you was to put her nose in your cupped hands, flatten her ears and gaze at you with soft eyes. Or to seal around the floor, hind legs crouched, tail swinging, crying softly in an agony of greeting, longing to show you how much she cared and how much she valued you.

Puma too was determined to prove that you should never generalise about dogs.

She should have died of lead poisoning. The pups licked paint that no one knew had lead in it. Porky died; Panther and Puma nearly died. Pan died at six of kidney failure due to the lead.

Puma had pups and had several complications that should have killed her. They didn't. She went septic after the pups, due to a jammed puppy. She developed a pyometra and nearly died of that. She recovered to live another seven years. I am still meeting her great-grandpuppies now.

Sadly, Puma did have brain damage at the end. She would thrust her head into my hands, pushing against them, or against the settee or even the wall. I didn't realise she had a blinding headache.

She began to over-protect me; she couldn't see who was there and would lunge at them, and try to nip. She barked at the slightest sound, which triggered the other dogs. Then the attacks became real, and we had to say goodbye.

I never realised, until the day after she died, how noisy she had been.

It was weeks before I stopped cutting everything into three, and remembered I only needed to make up two meals now.

Those are dog days too; days to be endured.

Janus was ten when Puma died. A very active ten-year-old, full of fun still. He had long ago learned what our signals meant, and the way to get him to come was to throw a toy, when he bolted to fetch it. He loved carrying my gloves and I always had to have three in my pocket, or he'd strip one off and leave my hand cold.

He could never resist small objects. He would carry my purse into the garden; I had to be sure it was out of his reach. He would raid the garage and I would be accused of having borrowed a screw driver and not returned it. So I took the dogs out to search for it. It was always out there, in the long grass, where our old dog had 'buried' it. You could tell from the daft expression on his face he thought this caper very funny.

Two dogs are easier than three, but not when one is my jealous Chita. She has to be Prima Donna, and she tried to boss Janus. He roared at her, and kept her in her place.

They had to be separated in the car. So I adopted Charlie Wyant's idea of two rings bolted into the floor, and a benching chain on each dog. If they were together they fought, and don't let anyone tell you dogs and bitches don't fight, as they do. Janus and Chita had to be watched, always. I could stop it, provided I was there; they didn't dare then. They were not left alone together until Janus was very old and had resigned his position. Yet, oddly, they were left together at night and there was never any trouble then.

Puma had bullied her brothers mercilessly when she was kennelled with them and had to be put by herself.

Two bitches don't necessarily fight either. Mind you, if they do decide to do so, it's almost incurable unless you are very masterful and never leave them alone together; and they fight like devils. Puma didn't really like Chita but she tolerated her, and they never had a single argument. By the time Chita was six months old, Puma had accepted the role of third dog in the pack, which prevented any trouble. She was a most unaggressive bitch.

The highlight of Puma's day was always her turn to walk alone with me; no other dog. Only dog. Lovely. All the attention just for her. She'd walk close, to feel safe as she couldn't see, and nuzzle me every now and then with her nose.

I knew how she felt. I had had to share my mother with three others, and it was a rare joy to go out with her, when I was a child, all by myself!

The years go by too fast. Janus was ten; he was eleven; he was twelve. He still had his forty-minute walk, although it was a very slow walk now. Chita had to pace him, heeling beside me, slowly. If I let them off she raced at him and knocked him off his legs, which were now becoming shaky.

On two occasions they almost gave way altogether when we were out. He cried if left at home. However, he would lie in the car after his walk while I trained Chita and she could race after her quoit, or have other games with me.

Chita always has so much surplus energy that she needs a great deal more training and exercise than the vast majority of dogs. Those of us with dogs like Chita have to accept that our lives are governed by the need to be Boss, all the time. Relax, and the dog will take over that role and make life a misery by being totally uncontrollable at all times.

One of the major difficulties, I find, in teaching new owners, is that they don't understand the role training plays in the human/canine partnership. Training teaches the dog how to control itself; give a command, like SIT, the dog obeys, and an undesirable action, like chasing a cat, is aborted.

33

Training lessons consolidate the bond between dog and owner: they are cooperating in something that is for their mutual benefit. The dog is told to sit, to lie down, to stand, and to come on command; to walk properly on the lead; to stay where he is told until he is told he may move. These exercises can all save his life in the right circumstances.

'Don't move; there's a car coming,' and the dog remains in the sit position at the kerb.

'Walk slowly, it's icy,' and dog and owner walk sedately, so no bones are broken.

Every time that command is enforced, the dog is being shown nicely that *you* are in control, you are Boss; every time it is disobeyed, he's showing you he doesn't give a damn about you; he will do exactly as he chooses and you can go suck a lollipop.

You have the unruly pup, and by about eight months he is biddable; and then he matures and tests you out. That is when training *really* begins. That is when clubs lose unhappy owners who are sure they've been sold down the river and training doesn't work. Up to now they haven't had to exert *real* authority, now they must. Up to now it's been child's play as you are so big and strong and godlike to your little cuddly pup. You are gentle and loving and he is responsive.

At eight months old the situation changes. He matures. If he were human he would probably now join the Communist party, take to trying strong drink and see how far he could go without provoking his parents to drastic measures. He is a big fellow, with ideas of his own, like finding a pretty little bitch and giving her pups. The battle is now on.

You have to prove that you are stronger. With some dogs, it's easy. With some it means a constant firm hand, never relaxing. With some you must use methods that owners of most dogs would regard as cruel. Which is more cruel – to allow the tearaway, as this type of dog is a villain, to get away with terrorising humans, as he will, ending in serious biting and probably his death by injection, or to establish authority and show him that no matter what *he* does, *you* have the upper hand?

Many dogs have been put to sleep who might have survived if

the owners had been shown the right way to teach *that* dog; not methods that worked with little submissive dogs of quite another character.

Many submissive pups become dominant at maturity; many quite horrible pups become more biddable. There are no rules at all, you learn with every dog. And where most people learn with one or two I learn with sixty or more different dogs every week; some come for ten weeks, some for twenty and some for thirty; I learn most from those.

If a certain method is preferable to death and will have an effect, then it should be used, briefly, under the supervision of a trained expert (and I don't mean a cowboy; ask a lot of questions before you trust your dog to a so-called 'trainer'). Provided the owner can exert authority for the rest of the dog's life, after the initial lesson, then the method used will work, done properly. If not, then the partnership is dangerous.

Which is preferable if a dog were to kill sheep – a bullet from the farmer, or half an hour's discomfort teaching him that whenever he goes near a sheep something very unpleasant indeed will happen?

In the past ten years I must have had five hundred dogs through the club. Three club dogs have killed sheep. All three were of different breeds; it isn't a crime that is committed by only one breed.

The first got out three times, and killed five in all. They don't kill quickly; they tear the gut or throat open, and then feed on the live animal. Nasty? Yes, but since more than 12,000 sheep are mauled each year by dogs, then it's necessary to say. The dog is a very brutal killer when it takes to killing; as savage as any fox.

The farmer offered the owner a choice. Death by bullet, or a kinder death from the vet, or sell her to a town home. I drove owner and bitch to have the bitch put down. She was fourteen months old.

I don't want a repetition of that day.

The second escaped from his owner as she was coming home from shopping, carrying handbag, shopping bag and with her big strong dog on a lead. He smelled sheep, pulled free and was over the fence in a flash. She watched, appalled, as he began to chivvy the sheep. She raced home for her own gun, hoping that if she fired it he might be so startled he would leave them. The police were called. The dog was finally caught. It had not killed, but in-lamb ewes can lose their lambs if chased by a dog. That's a great deal of money gone down the drain, and a great deal of misery incurred.

The dog was sold to a city home where there are no sheep and the owner was let off with a caution as she was prepared to take drastic measures herself to end the terror for the sheep.

The third was allowed to wander by himself. I knew what would happen and it did. He arrived home one day pouring blood from a bullet in the gut; he had dragged himself for miles, to get back to comfort and safety. He had been seen repeatedly in the sheep field, chasing. He was out, alone, with no supervision and he was a big tough dog. He was a lovely fellow. He died, in agony, before the vet arrived.

I do *not* blame the farmer. Not only are sheep his livelihood, but any sheep that is mauled is also a living animal and it suffers terribly. I've lived among sheep for ten years now and they are far from stupid creatures.

My farmer neighbours breed sheep and if my dog gets out and into the sheep field, and is shot, then it's *my* fault. We have sheep in the fields on both sides and I am always out with my dogs even when they are in our own garden.

I get very irritated by people who say: 'The dog gets out; I can't stop him.' Dogs can't get through closed doors; and if the dog is a wanderer then the owner should build a safe kennel and pen and put him there whenever too busy to supervise. Or not have a dog at all. We have a 2-acre paddock but I also have a safe pen. I don't think dogs should be left out in gardens alone. People leave gates open; walls are jumpable; hedges aren't always dog-proof.

So much depends on the dogs and people involved. You can't lay down a rigid law, ever. But if we have dogs we have a major responsibility to see that they do not harry our neighbours; do not chase sheep, cats, rabbits or children; do not get free and cause a road accident, when human lives may be lost.

We also have to accept that dogs grow old faster than humans. Thirteen years is a good age, and most of us will live beyond that. Our lives will, if we are genuinely dog-orientated, contain a progression of dogs, and their memories.

Each dog adds to our experience and provides more knowledge, so that we don't make the same mistakes with our last dog as we made with our first.

We might make different mistakes! Nobody's perfect.

I have very little time, either, for those who sell off their old dogs because they aren't producing, or working and cost too much to keep. I was told by several very experienced breeders to ask, when I went to a Kennels, to see the veterans, the old retired dogs. If there aren't any, don't buy, as the same uncaring attitude will be given to puppy rearing: cut corners, keep costs down, get our money back.

Many people use dogs; many people abuse dogs. Some years ago I met a lovely bitch aged about ten years old. Her owners had had her for three years. They had found her lying in the gutter, having been dumped from a car. She was full of milk. The vet, examining her, said she was exhausted. She must have had a litter every season since her first. Now she was thrown away.

One of my friends has a champion Foreign Lilac cat whose son proved capable of winning more prizes than she so she was given to a cat sanctuary. She was lucky as she has a much more caring home now. She is valued for herself alone, as she isn't shown.

I find myself, more and more, analysing people by the way they behave with their dogs. Sell off the old ones, the useless breeding stock, or put them down. Put down a dog because it isn't winning. One source of six- to eight-month-old pups is the breeder who runs pups on to see if they will win. They don't and then they come on the market, but not everybody wants a kennel-kept dog that is no longer a puppy, and some of these end up unhappily. I cannot bear to see a dog that has been part of the family and lived in the house, or worked hard at stud, or producing pups, or in competitions and won awards, put down to make way for a newcomer that is more likely to win prizes.

It may seem sentimental but if so one of my favourite people, Eric Roberts, is also sentimental. He has trained dogs for most of his life; he trains protection dogs and finds dogs for the police. A lot of people might regard him as ultra-tough. Yet when I first knew him, some years ago, his dog Callan was still alive. Callan was living out his old age in his home surroundings, a cherished dog, who when the final crunch came, died in the arms of the master he'd worked for so many years before. He was then fourteen.

'He worked well for me,' Eric said. His business was founded on Callan and his Kennels is named Callanway. 'He deserved to live out his life in a happy old age.'

The old dog came for walks with us. He hated being left at home, but at times his legs gave way, and he had to be carried back, often holding a stone in his mouth that he had picked up. Callan loved carrying stones, right up to his last few days of life. He was a wonderful character and a lovely old dog.

Sometimes when I go to Trials I stay with a friend and his wife. He is a police sergeant; again a big tough man, in charge of training police dog handlers and their dogs. Part of the family, every time I visited up to the last, has been his retired police dog. The old dog was now a pet; his legs were going and he was deaf, but he loved his food, and his owners, and his little walks each day. He died last year. Like Callan, he was well over twelve years old, which is a remarkable age for a German Shepherd. Both had been working dogs.

I learned all about the problems of old dogs with Janus. We did not have to adjust to deafness; that had been done many years before, so I had a bonus. We did have to adjust to his wobbly hindlegs that sometimes gave way. Chita thought it funny to barge him and knock him over; he was now second dog, no longer wanting to challenge her, and after this had happened twice I knew he had to come out alone with me in the garden. Brash young miss would have to stay indoors and yell, which she did, every time.

Walks became little potters, Janus trotting along at an old dog's pace, still loving every minute, finding wonderful smells, lolloping if he saw a rabbit, miles behind it, never in any danger of catching it. He no longer felt he had to obey me. Chita did have to obey; she would have caught the rabbit and I wasn't having that tormented by my dog. It had feelings too.

After Chita had had her training, he climbed out of the car, arranged himself at heel and looked at me.

'My turn now.'

So we did a few steps of heelwork, and then I threw the dumbbell for him. That was always the highlight of any training session; Janus was born to retrieve. Honour satisfied, he went to sit by the car and look at me.

'Lift me in.'

He could no longer jump up from the ground into the back of my estate car.

Injections helped him for a few weeks and then the trouble would recur, always unpredictably. He would be fine for days, and want his walks, and plead to go on longer. My vet said let him try; it will give him an interest in life.

It did, however, catch me out on two occasions.

Chapter Four

Our first hint of what was to come happened late in autumn at the Botanic gardens beside the Menai Straits. We had walked along the cliff path and through the playing fields, only to find the gate padlocked on our return, as our walk had taken far longer than I had expected. It was dusk; Janus had had to have two long rests. He had walked that so easily before, even the week before, but today was another step towards the end. It was too far. We could no longer take that walk together.

In another few weeks he would be thirteen years old. My vets had said he would never make three; I had had a ten-year bonus.

Now I knew that each day his horizons would become more restricted. Those hind legs were refusing their job, and beginning to drag. I could never subject him to total indignity. One day, the decision would have to be mine. It was sad to know that we would now have to abandon a route we all loved: I had the views over the Straits, and the dogs had the most wonderful smells.

I looked at my old dog, and patted his head. He grinned up at me, his eyes still bright with mischief, although he was very tired. For the moment I would enjoy him, and not count the days.

I had forgotten his glove, which was his 'pheasant', and he hadn't found a stick. He butted my hand and stripped off my glove, shook it and settled it comfortably in his mouth. He looked at me. 'Forgot, didn't you? OK, be cold.' He turned back the way we had come, knowing we couldn't get through that gate.

I could climb the gate. I couldn't lift Janus over. He couldn't climb it. Chita could have jumped it easily. There was another gate in the wood and that might not be locked. It was now nearly dark. Nobody was about. The car was two hundred yards away, on the other side of a chained five-barred gate.

We had to find our way through the woods. In the dark. We blundered and crashed and then the ground suddenly gave way and I plunged painfully down a bank into brambles. I held on to Chita, but dropped Janus's lead, and he, at that moment, saw a rabbit.

He took off!

I heard him blundering along and, with Chita on lead, I followed. We caught him easily enough, but we were now further than ever from the second gate. It was almost dark and as we pushed through brambles to find the path, which Janus had left, it became quite dark.

If I fell, we would be in real trouble as the place was so isolated. No one would come down at night. They would find my car in the morning and then there would be a search party, but ...

It didn't bear thinking about.

Owls called. It was very isolated and the rustling trees were spooky. I could imagine unseen antagonists, human, animal, and maybe even werewolf, lurking there! We finally made the path, and kept to it, with so little light that only my feet told me where I was. The ground I walked on was hard-packed mud. Luckily it hadn't been raining. When it has, the going is lethal: slippery mud all the way, and a gentle downwards slope.

At last we made the gate, which was, fortunately, not padlocked, and climbed on to a gravel path leading upwards and out by the houses, to walk back to my car which was parked in a little lane some distance away. We had to take it slowly. I was cursing myself because Janus was now very tired indeed.

We had walked more than twice as far as I intended.

Chita, of course, was still frisky. She hadn't had her extra-fast training games and was full of energy.

After what seemed an age, as we had to stop every few paces and let Janus lie down and recover his energy, we reached the car. One thing, no other idiot would be out in the dark with a

41

dog and I could at least relax, and put Chita on to a downstay while I lifted Janus, who had collapsed by the car and was a dead weight.

If other dogs come she has to protect us and all thought of staying still and being good is forgotten. Normally she went in to the car first and was tied till I had Janus in, but she screamed with what could be frustration, impatience or temper if I did that. (I know now it's her breeding. I've had over thirty in club bred on similar lines, and every one has been a screamer.)

I told Chita to stay in the down. I don't use the word stay as everybody uses it and someone may tell my dog to stay, not meaning that at all. She had the command and her hand signal. Normally that works very well, so long as she isn't at Trials when it's a very different story. If I put her in the car first she always had a little go at Janus, and I didn't want him harassed.

I picked him up, a remarkably heavy armful as he weighed eighty pounds and was by now unable to help himself at all. Just as I leaned forward to put him in the car, an ex club member appeared with her dog. Chita saw the dog and raced at it. No dog had a right to be there.

I shouted NO.

But Chita had had enough of being good. She had had to walk at an old dog's pace for over an hour and she was still full of fire and go. She charged. I put Janus down on his car rug, and left him. He was beyond moving.

The other dog, a charming Labrador, was standing rigid, as Chita raced at top speed down the path towards him, barking. She hit the ramp that is there to slow down cars, somersaulted, yelped and raced on. She barked again and I shouted to her, and at last she condescended to hear me. She reached me, pouring blood from a hole in her chin.

Not even that had stopped her.

I put her in the car, and apologised. I made friends again with the Labrador, a placid fellow, and we went our separate ways. I stopped off at the vet, as luckily it was surgery time. Janus had an injection to help his doddery legs, and Chita had her skinned chin bathed, the hole examined, probably made by a sharp stone, and also had an injection to combat infection.

For the next few weeks Kenneth took Janus out for a potter; Kenneth was recovering from a broken leg, due to falling over the old dog in the dark, when I was away at Trials a few months before with Chita. He had forgotten Janus's trick of lying right in the middle of the hall, between the front door and the light switch. Janus, being deaf, didn't hear him come and as Kenneth touched him with his foot, the dog jumped up and my poor husband went headlong. I found him lying in an armchair with a swollen leg, and suffering from severe shock, some hours later. He had fractured his ankle and his shin bone. After that we both took a lot more care when going into a dark room. So both of them were slow.

I took Chita out alone and trained her and we had a fast-pace walk. She is far more manageable on her own, as she needs all my concentration.

Then came a cold February day when Kenneth's leg was playing up and hurt him, so I took out both dogs. We went to our favourite walk at Newborough Warren. Janus seemed remarkably spry, and again it was a rabbit that was his undoing. Newborough is dune land. It was very much February Filldyke and the ground between the dunes was flooded.

The dogs didn't care.

They romped up the grass-covered sandy slopes, and skidded down the other side. For once, Chita behaved and was off lead. Janus galloped around at his lumbering elderly pace, brought me sticks, took my glove, and grinned all over. He was out with me again. I saw another dog and leashed my little chaser, but left the old dog free. He could do no harm. Chita never has done more than bark when she reaches the object of her chase, but if the other dog reacted she might fight. She loathes dogs that run free and race at her, barking. Come to that, so do I.

I know her habit well and if I see another dog I do leash her, and I wish others would do the same. I don't always see a dog appear behind me. Chita has eyes in the back of her head!

I didn't see the rabbit till too late. Janus was off, at a sedate trot, but too fast for me to catch. No use calling, he couldn't hear. Chita and I ran after him. The end came soon, as his legs collapsed completely, and he lay, panting heavily, quite unable to move, in a wet patch.

I dragged him up one of the dunes till he was on dry ground. The car was in sight from the dune top but there were three more dunes in between, and water all round the foot of the sandhills. It was remarkably cold.

All would have been well if it hadn't been for the rabbit. I had thought he was too old to chase; as usual, my dog proved me wrong.

We sat for half an hour, Chita whining. Janus put his head on my knee and looked at me. I stroked him gently, wondering if I could get him to the car. I could never carry him.

At last he struggled to move, got up on his front legs and dragged his hind legs. He knew we had to get home. Besides, it was coming on for his dinner time, at five o'clock. I took off my scarf, looped it under his tummy to take the weight of his hind end, and we set off, Janus scrambling gamely, stopping every few yards to collapse, and so did I, as I had much of his weight on my arms. Chita now sounded like a banshee, horrified at the way we were progressing.

I needed help but didn't want anyone to see us, with one dog being dragged up one side of the dunes and slid down the other, and another dog screaming like a maniac and pulling on her lead, which was now anchored round my waist to leave both hands free for Janus. I dared not let her off. Suppose *she* saw a rabbit?

By now my arms were aching, I was panting, my chest hurt, and I wondered if I was going to have a heart attack! That was all we needed. We moved a few yards at a time, and then both of us collapsed, and Chita had to lie still. She could continue to complain miserably for all that, and did so. I knew just how she felt, but making noises was no help whatsoever.

After an hour and a half we were about fifty yards from the car. I could lug Janus up the last dune and slide him down, or navigate the water. Going up and down would add at least a hundred yards; I chose the flooded ground. I was becoming exhausted too. At one point we both collapsed into the water. I no longer cared.

We were all wet when we reached the car. Janus dropped beside it and lay quite still. Chita leaped in fast and glared at me. She'd never had a walk like it. Nor had I for that matter. It was some minutes before I had enough energy to lift Janus, who felt as if he were dead, into the car. I towelled him vigorously, laid him on his rug and put my coat over him. I always have a spare warm anorak in the car.

It was another half hour before I had enough energy to start driving. I switched on the radio and just sat. Once I started, I stopped twice to look back at Janus. I wasn't sure whether he was asleep or dead.

We reached the vet's. They know me well as Janus had to have an additive for his pancreas deficiency all his life, and we called in every fortnight for seven years.

It made some people think I had remarkably unhealthy dogs!

I went in and told the nurse what had happened.

'Poor old boy,' she said. 'Bring him in and let's lie him by the Aga. Both vets are out on visits, but they'll be back soon.'

We carried Janus in. He watched us, but he had no energy left to move. He lay on a rug by the warm stove, and we had coffee. He responded to our voices, and wagged his tail. That was all.

Then it was time to feed the four cats belonging to the practice: two lovely marmalade cats named Polly and Topsy and two pretty grey-and-whites named Tiddles and Tish. Food was put in four bowls and four cats walked round exclaiming. Neither of us noticed that Janus had raised his head and was watching them closely.

Janus, in his old age, had become very greedy. Before we had time to stop him, he was up and tucking in, while a deprived cat screamed in fury. I removed my dog, puss's bowl was topped up and all was peace once more. Janus decided to go walkabout.

He walked round the hospital room where he had been lying; out into the waiting room, to and fro, to and fro, slowly, carefully, and then faster, until when the vet arrived, he was walking almost normally and my story was laughed at, kindly.

I took him home. He was now a very old dog indeed. His muzzle was grey; his movements were ponderous, and those wretched legs failed him more and more often. He had to be helped into the garden; and he didn't always make it. His walks became little potters, and he followed the sun round the house, as if knowing it would ease his stiff legs.

Out with me, alone, he would do a little frisk for his quoit and fetch it. Once was enough; honour was satisfied. Most of the time he lay asleep, dreaming an old dog's dreams. Chita left him alone now.

Then came a Saturday morning when those legs wouldn't work at all. He was too heavy to drag out into the garden.

I rang the vet.

'I think the time has come,' I said.

He came out, and agreed with me.

I held Janus for the last time. I took Chita to say goodbye so that she didn't search for him endlessly, not knowing where he had gone. We stood together looking at my game old dog. He lay as if asleep, the sun shining on his golden coat. I hoped he had joined Puma and that they were running together in green fields by a river as they had loved to run when young.

Then I took Chita for a very long walk. Well away from all our favourite places.

I didn't go back to our favourite walk at Newborough for almost a year. Kenneth and I walked Chita there on Boxing Day, and the whole way I was haunted by my two old dogs. How they had loved the forest, running ahead, sniffing at the verges beside the road, checking constantly to make sure we were following. Chita was sober that day, almost as if she too remembered days long past, days never to be recaptured.

As I write, it is now almost a year since Janus died, but his memory is as vivid as ever. His rosettes hang on the wall and so do the photographs of him; holding his dumbbell; running with a broom which he couldn't quite manage; and a lovely head study which appears in this book. It was taken by Seán Hagerty,

46

who photographs my dogs, just before Janus died, as I knew that would be all I had to remember him by soon.

The memories now are kind; days of pleasure and days of laughter. The young Golden Retrievers that come to club so often do something that triggers memory and I stand for a moment, forgetting what I was about to say, with a sudden lump in my throat.

Janus did that too, when he was a pup. You lucky, lucky people, with all those years ahead. My years with Janus are over.

It feels like the end of an era.

Janus taught me so much.

I can pass on what he taught me to others, so he has left a permanent memorial. Chita will leave that too. One day, in what I hope is the far future.

She will leave an even bigger gap, as after Janus died, she became closer to me than any dog I have ever had.

Kipling, who had dogs too, was so right when he said: 'Brothers and sisters, I bid you beware of giving your heart to a dog to tear.'

Those who never have dogs will never know what they have missed; or what we feel.

Our dogs' lives may be short, but it is we who are privileged.

Sleep well, soldier. We'll never forget you, my brave old dog.

Chapter Five

It took time to get used to life without Janus. Even in his old age he was a terrific character, and had been Kenneth's constant companion for the last two years. Travelling had proved uncomfortable for the old dog, so that he stayed at home when we went to Trials. He couldn't cope with stairs either in hotels and motels.

But Chita, being Chita, revelled in being the only dog. She no longer had to exert her dominance at home; no dog challenged her – and even up to his last days Janus did sometimes tell her off.

'Leave me in peace, pest.'

She became far more relaxed at home, although I doubt if she ever will relax when away from home. She is always on the *Qui vive.*? Who goes there? On guard. I know now this is her breeding. I have had so many in club bred on similar lines to her dam's lines, and they are often nervous, invariably noisy, squealing with excitement or panic, or just plain restlessness, and very alert indeed, sometimes to the point of tackling other dogs when there has been no challenge whatever. Some are very anxious and apt to run away, or hide between chairs.

Nowadays the dogs that make Chita as she is may be doubled or trebled and I do wish breeders would stop and *think*. Our last two bred that way joined recently. The puppy squeals more or less non-stop, and becomes agitated at things that don't upset the other pups at all; and the eight-month-old dog, a big fellow, stands and trembles, and dives behind chairs for shelter.

Our other German Shepherds, bred on different lines, or with one of these dogs alone only once, are very nice indeed.

It does create such problems for owners, especially new owners who have their first dog and are totally bewildered.

Over protection is a bad idea for these dogs. They need calm, very considerate, matter-of-fact handling and you must never, never shout at them.

The maxim 'it's the owner, not the dog,' only applies in that if the owner were experienced these faults could be overcome. New owners don't know how to correct them and how to give the dog the confidence it needs. The right dog club may help, but dog club instructors can't live with the dog and watch the owner at home. My experiences with Janus and Puma enabled me to keep Chita. Had she been my first dog ever, she would not be here. As it was, I had many doubts during those first two years with her.

Each dog teaches you a great deal. Coping with a deaf dog taught me about all kinds of dogs, as Janus's disability seemed to be that of stupidity. He was actually extremely clever and covered up so well that he foxed even experts, who didn't believe he was deaf.

He could lip read. Say 'Cheese' and he knew what we were talking about and ran to the fridge, all eagerness. Dogs read us all the time, so walking shoes, lead, bowl out of the cupboard, walk to the dogfood bag, never need any explanation to either a hearing or a deaf dog.

Puma's lead poisoning turned her into a zombie. She had to be coaxed out of it. She had to be treated like a mentally handicapped child, and patterned, by repetition of every exercise, over and over again. Everything a normal dog learns took ten times as long to teach Puma, but once she began to respond, she was so delighted when she had a new achievement, that it was worth all the struggling.

Her two third prizes in Obedience took much more effort than did her Breed prizes for beauty.

Now, with Chita, I was learning yet another new discipline, as she is my first Working Trial dog. Janus was dysplastic, with a faulty hip, so he couldn't jump. There was no way Puma could have worked in Trials: she needed me beside her all the time or she had no confidence. The pups had been isolated from the world from five months old for eleven weeks; lead poisoning can be a killer, and usually is. The pups had to be kept in the dark. Even then she went blind at seven, due to that long-ago accident. The first few months are very important in a dog's life, when it should be taken out and about to meet people and other dogs. Luckily she was always safe with other dogs, but she was anxious about people.

She didn't come to live with me till she was seventeen months old, as my father was dying of cancer, so that she had a lot of readjustments to make. She had lived, till she came home with me, in a kennel. She found the house terrifying at first.

She had to be reassured and gentled, and those weeks with her were of inestimable value when it came to taming Chita. Puma hadn't been fierce. Chita's ferocity was due to terror. Somehow, in the first important eight weeks of her life, she hadn't learned to trust humans or dogs. With a litter of strong-minded pups, those not so dominant can well be shouldered out by the bold ones, and bullied by them, and lose in socialising as they don't come first to be fed, or to see people.

By the time Janus had died, Chita and I knew more about Trials, but I didn't know nearly enough. I had much more time to spare, with only one dog. I would now learn more.

All the old hands tell me I can learn to track on my own tracks. Maybe they can learn to track on *their* own tracks. There is so much to learn as it isn't just a case of following the dog. You have to be thinking all the time, working out what she is doing; is she tracking, or is there a strange scent, such as sheep scent, distracting her? Is she ground-scenting, or, nose-up, taking a breath, and not distracted at all? Just relaxing after a few yards of intense concentration, her nose almost digging into the earth.

I can't learn only from my own tracks. I know where they go, and don't watch the dog so closely as on a track I haven't seen laid. I can't see the footsteps in the grass. I don't know if I am dumb or what, but I learn little when I know where the track goes. I desperately needed someone to lay me tracks when I wasn't there. Get out on that competition field of grass or

50

plough, or stubble, and see nothing whatever in any direction but those two poles that tell you the first leg is there, and I am totally at sea.

I needed Eric Roberts on my doorstep, not 120 miles away, or on the phone.

That was impossible. I was beginning to feel I could never progress, I had no one to help me, so maybe I needed a complete change of direction, and forget about Trialling. There was the dog club. Perhaps I could expand that.

Soon after Janus died I felt I needed a change badly. Not Trials, but a day watching Eric train his problem dogs. This would help me gain knowledge, and might help me know what to do with dogs that have real problems, so long as they don't bite.

So I booked in with Chita at my home-from-home, the Ellesmere Hotel, Macclesfield, where the two Angelas are friendly and the food is splendid. We have the downstairs room by the fire escape, and can get out to the garden without going through the public rooms. They now have the most gorgeous little bitch, another German Shepherd, that Eric found and trained for them. Much easier than my Chita. I don't dare let them meet as Chita has stayed there for three years now, often, and tends to regard it as her territory. She might argue. She spent a lot of time sniffing under the bedroom door at the corridor knowing there was another bitch around.

That hotel holds some odd memories. On one occasion a trade delegation was there from Red China. Men and women in a kind of uniform. They asked to take over the kitchen to prepare a Chinese meal on their last evening. The meal was very splendid, and the two Angelas were invited to join in the feasting. The rest of us had to sit and wait till everyone had eaten. I got remarkably hungry, watching everyone else eat. The food looked and smelled and apparently also tasted delicious.

On another occasion, the year before, I woke very early to hear a police car driver speaking through his tannoy.

'There is a black cloud of chemicals approaching. Shut all

51

doors and windows, and do not go outside until you are told it is safe to do so.'

I looked out of my window as I shut it and saw a pall of dense black smoke over Macclesfield. I grabbed my dressing gown and went out, to find blonde Angela busy knocking on doors. She asked me to go and knock too, and I spent an odd half-hour banging on the doors of total strangers till I heard voices, and repeating the police message.

Suppose Chita needed to go outside?

I could see the smoke from my bed. What was it? Suppose we had to evacuate? I had not seen anything like it since the war and it had to be a major fire.

I dressed and went to sit in the dining room with Chita on her lead, and a book to read, but it was hard to concentrate. There was a police car parked next door, turning all the traffic back, and diverting it round Macclesfield; fire engine sirens sounded; police car sirens sounded; there seemed to be ambulances too, though I didn't see them.

Afterwards I realised there had been the most splendid police organisation.

The police cars continued to warn us to stay indoors. We had breakfast, marooned, no one quite knowing what to do. I should have been walking Chita and then going up to Eric. We were to have a tracking lesson that time. Nobody could leave; the rest should all have been driving off to appointments. The phone was kept busy as people had to ring and notify those expecting them they would be late if they came at all.

Luckily Eric was in the opposite direction to the fire. I could get out of town; it was unlikely I could get through it. At one point the hotel was lost in a thick black fog.

Then the wind changed and we were told we were free to go, just before ten o'clock.

Chita was bursting.

I took her for a walk that was much shorter than I anticipated as the air was vile, and we were both beginning to choke. My throat and lungs felt raw after just a few minutes. I turned back, took my car, hoping it hadn't been affected by the smoke,

52

especially as I had only had it a week and it was brand new, and drove up to Eric's.

Up is the operative word as he is high above Macclesfield in wonderful clear air and he hadn't seen or heard anything about the fire, although when I pointed out the smoke he could see it as it lay like a thick black pall over the industrial estate which is about half a mile from the hotel.

By evening we knew that Macclesfield had been the scene of a huge fire-fighting exercise. They had had 80 firemen, from Cheshire, Derbyshire, Staffordshire and Manchester, according to the local papers. They had had ten pumps and the Chemical Unit Incident vans. When I left next day there were still hoses down the streets leading to the estate, a diversion, to keep people away, and the fire, though well under control, was still causing problems.

The fumes were the worst part of it, as people had sore throats and chests afterwards; mine stayed sore for about three days. They managed marvellously as no one was seriously injured, although seven firemen had to go to hospital for checks.

The factory made PVC granules and the powder components and some solvents had caught fire.

I spent a fascinating day with Eric and by the time I got back to the hotel all was quiet again. That was the last day I spent there until after Janus died. There was little sign of the fire when I drove back eight months later for my special dog day, although I remembered that night as I looked from my window out over Macclesfield and down towards the industrial estate.

There would be another difference too: it would be the first time that I reached home in thirteen years without Janus waiting eagerly to greet me, holding a present for me, wagging all over and groaning with delight because we had come back to him. Even Chita behaved at those meetings, and greeted him happily, nose to nose.

It was a sad year. My friend Joy lost both Glenn and Pepper, her Shelties, who were Janus's contemporaries; Eric lost his old GSD Callan, and the friends I stay with for one Trials had lost old Van, also a GSD. One thing, we all knew how the others felt. All, except Joy, had other dogs.

That June day was one of the hottest of the year. Eric had put out a chair, so that I could sit and watch. Chita was in the shade, with the back of the car open to give her plenty of air. My car also has an awning for shade. She has a benching chain, could see me, and settled quietly to sleep.

Most of the dogs were newly in for problem curing, or for protection training.

The first was a pretty German Shepherd bitch who was more nervous than any I had ever seen. Eric told me to keep absolutely still. He sat on the ground, and let her wander. She was extremely unhappy, and obviously very afraid of people. He thought it was her breeding rather than her treatment as her owners were very concerned and had tried hard to help her.

He talked to her; softly, soothingly, happily, teasingly, gently, coaxingly. Gradually she came to him; she let him stroke her.

'Come on then. You aren't afraid of me, are you? There's a good girl.'

By the end of half an hour she had relaxed. Nobody had put a lead on her, nor a chain; nobody had made her do anything she didn't want to do. She came, very warily, to me. I spoke to her, and she nosed my hand. I spoke again softly and she let me touch her.

She had to relax before she could understand training. If she were tense she'd learn nothing. So her first week was to teach her to trust Eric; to be sure he would do nothing that would alarm her. That first half-hour was to inspire her confidence. She went home three weeks later a far happier little animal.

Training does help overcome nerves; but always in a dog like that, or in a dog like Chita, heredity will take over in any situation that puts the dog under stress. The only way to deal with it is to put them fast into a training situation with which they are totally familiar. I do a little heelwork with Chita and a few fast sits and she forgets the bogeymen now.

In club I do very little at first with nervous dogs. They come;

they get used to the place and the people and other dogs; they may sit at the side while other dogs and people pass them. I sit on the floor to talk to them; and when they greet me of their own free will, then they are ready to start to work. You can make them do it by corrective checks and terror but I think it is cruel and not very useful, as it does not help the dog overcome its fears; it merely makes it more scared of you and what you will do than what terrifies it, and I don't feel that is a good basis for living.

I do explain to owners what I do and why and that a great deal of dedication will be needed from them. Our rescued, badly treated dogs have done well. Our latest, a very nervous Dobe, is, after blotting her copybook by panic biting before she came to us, just beginning to work. Our little Gordon Setter that puddled if you raised your voice or moved toward her, comes to greet me. She looks down at the floor to make sure she hasn't puddled this time and her air of relief as she realises she really hasn't is endearingly comical. She was a very worried frightened little bitch at first.

We keep disinfectant and paper towels handy and there is a mop and bucket so a small sin doesn't matter. Any accident is so rare that it is memorable.

Eric's second dog that day was a big handsome German Shepherd that had come in for training for protection work. There was nothing wrong with his temperament. He came out of his kennel full of delight at being able to do something. As he had only recently come in, his lesson was to smarten up his obedience and his reactions, as a protection dog *must* be safe, above all else. It may have to find a confused old person, or a little child gone missing from a picnic, straying away from the family, as well as chase a hardened criminal who may have a gun. The dog must be one hundred per cent reliable. No hit-and-miss and hope here.

Eric, like many good dog trainers, and horsemen too, is slightly built, though very muscular, and not quite six feet tall, which probably helps give dogs confidence as they don't like being towered over. Watching him I was reminded of my first dog lesson ever, about 1960, given by an experienced dog handler.

I had gone out, on a bitterly cold January morning, to report on the training of police dogs for *Scout* magazine. It was so cold and the ground so freezing that we had frequent cups of coffee, brewed on a primus, and took turns to sit by the primus to warm our hands.

I was too cold to make notes so had to rely on my memory which luckily is very good.

The men were told to put their dogs back in the vans.

Then we were all told to get down on all fours. A very tall inspector charged past us, loomed over us, giving us a dog's eye view of a giant, apparently threatening us all.

'Where is your horizon?' we were asked.

My view was blocked by a small bush that I hadn't bothered about when I was standing erect; now it looked enormous and I couldn't see beyond it. There might have been lakes, seas, wolves, or tigers, for all I knew from where I crouched. We spent some time discussing the limitations of the dog's eye view: he didn't know what was over the wall, although we did.

The dog had to learn to trust us so implicitly that he would obey every command, whether he was able to see for himself or had to act in blind faith. Often our dogs do act in blind faith, as they have no way of telling what lies beyond an opening. We know; we can see, or past experience tells us. We take our dogs into places they have not been to before, into situations they have never met before and expect them to behave as we do.

We are surprised when they don't.

How do we feel going for the first time into a new experience? A meeting of total strangers and you want to join the club; the first day at school; opening a door into a room we have never seen before.

That long-ago learning experience stood me in good stead last year when I was told to send Chita away to the horizon. I did, and dropped her. The judge said: 'That's *not* the horizon.'

I looked up at him. He was six foot three; I am five foot one. I suggested he came down to my height. He stared at me, and bent his knees and looked.

'It is your horizon,' he said. 'Now you have set me a problem as I can't do anything but give you almost full marks as she did make a mistake. But others must have been your height. I hadn't thought about it.'

Watching Eric, I could see that he often stopped and considered the dog; considered what it could see, what it was doing, and why. It wasn't just a case of following a set pattern for all dogs. Talking about each afterwards reenforced this opinion. He knew the dog's history; what triggered it to misbehave (and that is different with every dog) and how soon he could start training, as all dogs differ again and you can't train a dog that doesn't know you at all. That is asking for trouble.

He stopped, too, to explain to me why he did certain things. 'This dog is coming up to off-lead work but isn't yet entirely reliable so I put a long line on him; if he does try to bolt, I have a chance to pick up the line and stop him. I can't reach him any other way.'

The field he works in is long, narrow and sloping so that he walks down hill and up hill all day, which must make him remarkably fit. Each dog has a half-hour lesson. The more experienced might have two, well apart. It is in the Peak District, in the Teg's Nose country park, so that there are lovely views and wide open spaces, and all the park for walking dogs.

There are hazards. Three years ago Chita was working there and we walked our dogs, and she began to vomit at lunchtime. I had to take her home, very ill, and in the night she vomited blood. One vet suspected she had eaten grass on which a primus stove had spilled and had paraffin poisoning. The two dogs of Eric's that were with her were also ill. It might have been a germ; but they had all been running free in the same area. I now watch her when we walk there.

Humans have some unpleasant habits and rarely consider animals. Mouldy sandwiches may lie around; there may be broken glass or open cans with jagged edges and food remains inside; all extremely harmful to an innocent animal unaware of danger.

Eric's next pupil was a Great Dane that was very dominant indeed. He did as he chose at home, and his owners were getting worried by him. He was a big beautiful fellow, and at that stage he was not going to do as Eric asked. He hadn't been in long, so there was no compulsion at all. The dog wandered round the field, ignoring calls to come. By the end of half an hour he was rather tired of doing nothing in particular and came and accepted the lead and chain. He had a short, very relaxed, extremely good tempered lesson, with loads of happy praise; an enthusiastic 'good lad' every time he did right.

He enjoyed that, and when I rang Eric some weeks later, I was told he had gone home a very different dog.

It is very difficult to make owners understand that it isn't food and bed and warmth and petting and fussing and letting him do as he chooses that binds your dog to you; it is telling him what to do, and when to do it, making sure he always does as he is told and as you wish, that means you are Boss. Every dog needs a leader to follow, a hero to worship. Even the dominant fellow will respect an owner who is stronger minded than he is. A dog can't worship someone who doesn't give a damn whether he does as he is told or not. He despises them, and knows very well he can get away with murder if he chooses.

'My dog won't let me touch his food, or his bed, or his toys, or if he gets on my bed I can't get him off,' people say.

Why on earth did they let that tiny morsel of life ever start such habits? We are so much bigger and stronger than the puppy; he must learn then that he does as he is told or humans won't like it. The answer is not to smack him. Once I nearly smacked a small girl who came in with her mother and a lovely big German Shepherd and kept smacking his face. That is unpardonable behaviour. The dog was doing nothing wrong, but he was unhappy as here he was in a new situation with lots of new people and other dogs and he was getting no consideration at all from his owners.

He was dragged in and nobody spoke to him till I did. His

eyes brightened, as he recognised that here was someone who did know what a dog needed: a bit of friendly attention and some praise and reassurance. Some dogs never ever hear the words 'good boy', or 'good girl'. Just 'stupid dog' and a smack, or a yell that teaches them nothing as the owner doesn't understand how to teach a dog.

Many so-called instructors and trainers don't either.

I know several people besides Eric who spend their time remedying the appalling and expensive 'training' done by people cashing in on the desire for a trained protection dog. They don't *train* it; everyone who passes the dog is told to hit it; and by the time it goes out it's a raving maniac.

Anyone can advertise; there are no qualifications needed to set up as a trainer. Not even dog experience in some cases. I have been on two courses in the past twelve years when I discovered that those holding the courses had come into competition with a Collie, done some winning for a couple of years and, hey presto, they were experts. They had never handled any other breed and had only owned a dog for a short time.

I could have taught them a lot, but I held my tongue and after that asked a lot more questions before I parted with my money.

The next dog that day in Macclesfield was a Bulldog. He was an enchanting little character, full of determination and very affectionate, but he pulled like a steam train.

Eric's job was to persuade him not to. He made us both laugh, as he was a small clown and knew he was. He had to have more rests than the normal dog as the heat was causing him to pant far more than is usual with other breeds. Bulldogs can have difficulty with their breathing.

We broke for lunch and to exercise our own dogs. Chita couldn't believe that she was having a day off, a fun day with no training herself. We took them for a walk on the moors, and then returned to eat and talk over the morning's dogs. I had intended to leave at about four but I was so fascinated I stayed until seven.

The afternoon dogs were easier, most being in for pet training as they were very disobedient or didn't come when called. This is relatively simple at the start as you put the dog on a long line, call him to you and praise him when he comes, over and over, till coming to you is such a treat that he doesn't run off.

I am always amazed by competition instructors who say the dog doesn't need praise once he knows an exercise. He needs praise for pleasing you all his life, even when very experienced indeed – not so much praise then, but praise at the end of each session for trying hard.

With Chita's training, she needs encouraging when the going gets hard. 'Good girl, come on then, try harder; your trophy is hidden over there; good girl, aren't you super,' and her tail goes up and waves merrily, her attitude changes and she works with a will instead of with an effort.

'Why bother; she won't tell me I'm good even if I do it perfectly.'

It is the same with us; we work better for praise too. 'That was a lovely meal' is so rewarding, even if it is the ten thousandth or so you have cooked.

If I praise an owner for good work, I can see them preen; if they had a tail it would wag. Praise is the good handler's secret weapon. I don't know who first said that, but it is the truest thing there is in dog training.

One of the most interesting dogs that day was a fighting black Labrador. He came in almost impossible, unable to mix with other dogs at all, and driving his owners up the wall, as he was so likely to fly at any dog they met and mean business.

He had been in for a week.

His lesson was totally informal. Eric fetched his own dogs, Fons and Dusty, his daughter's little Collie and the two dogs belonging to his kennel manageress, Helen Sargent. Four German Shepherds and a Collie. They all knew one another well, and exercised together.

Out they came into the field, full of delight, and began to play.

In came black dog.

He looked at the other dogs and his hackles went up, very slightly.

'Down,' said Eric and all his and Helen's dogs went down and lay still. Black dog didn't quite know what to make of it. His hackles went down and the other dogs were released and began to play. By the end of half an hour he was not only playing too, but if Eric said 'Down', he went down with the other dogs. By the end of three weeks he was a reformed character.

So many people don't let their young dogs mix with people and dogs; this is how going to a good dog club can make so much difference.

We ended the day with a joint training session: Eric, Helen and myself, each of us working our own dogs, practising stays and giving them some freedom.

'You were late tonight,' said dark Angela as she served my meal. I had intended to be back at the hotel by five.

'I couldn't tear myself away,' I said. 'It was fascinating. All those dogs, all so different and Eric had a different method for each. It's helped me a lot.'

I didn't realise it at the time, but it had boosted my morale as so often those who think they know are so dogmatic. You don't do this. You don't do that. The dog is trained now. Don't bother to praise, it doesn't need it.

I know now that my methods with club dogs were right. We never have such problems as those Eric takes as you can't have the really difficult dog in club at all. You can't deal with all the little problems in exactly the same way. You can never start a nervous dog the very first time it comes by putting it on the floor with the other dogs and forcing it to learn the exercises. It can't learn; terror prevents it and owner and dog become frustrated and unhappy and leave. You have done more harm than good.

Some years ago I went on a course given by Charlie Wyant, the Grand Old Man of Obedience. One of his sayings I remember particularly:

'A dog that won't play won't work.'

In other words, until the dog is relaxed you can't teach it anything. I find that owners must also relax; tense people make tense dogs, and an unhappy team that can't progress. They are held back by their own fears.

61

The job of the club instructor is to relax dogs and owners as well, otherwise all their efforts are doomed to failure.

I want one hundred per cent success for every owner and every dog. I train, in my club, for daily living not for competition, and we have tests at the end of each twelve-week course. Last time out we averaged 92 per cent with thirty-two owners taking the tests. The pass mark is 80 per cent. It's worth aiming high. Why teach people to do it badly when we can teach them to do it well?

Chapter Six

Some years ago, when we lived in Cheshire, we had an extension built onto our house. The builder, a small dedicated man, always started off any conversation with me with the words: 'I've had a little think.'

One day his thoughts were about duchesses and princesses, which mystified me completely, as my only acquaintance with them is through reading about them. He, it appeared, was extremely familiar with them.

They were types of roofing tile!

Every branch of human activity develops its own jargon. Use the letters CC and, according to the company you are in, you may mean Chief Constable, or County Council, or Championship Certificate.

My aunt, who died last year at well over ninety, when very young was a secretary in the War Office. She made notes and had to read them back to a rather august company of high-ranking Army officers.

She read:

'Lloyd George took a permanent seat on the W.C.'

Her announcement was greeted with a gale of laughter and she never did live that incident down. The letters stood for War Cabinet.

In dogs, life is even more complex as each branch of training has its own jargon. When teaching our dogs to jump in Agility or in Working Trials, we say 'hup', which is a nice lifting word. But many gundog men say 'hup' instead of 'sit' – heaven knows why!

In the same way the exercise we call a sendaway they call a goback, and the dog is retrieving. I may have it wrong as I have found when talking to people who train gundogs that we don't

talk the same language and have many misunderstandings. I
am aware of them; they aren't, as mostly they don't delve as I do
into other forms of dog training.

However, I have no intention whatever of trying to teach
anyone to train a gundog. I do know my limitations. It doesn't
make me any less knowledgeable about my own forms of
training or about dogs.

I couldn't train a sheepdog to herd sheep either, although I
could teach him house manners and how to behave in public as
a companion dog.

So I may well be obscure to some people when I talk about
Obedience or Working Trials. Competition was a closed book
to me too until 1970, other than police dog trials, which were
run at Belle Vue in Manchester for many years and which I
watched from 1960 on.

There are so many kinds of show. There are the little fun
shows, known as Exemption shows, at which any dog may be
entered. There will be four classes for registered dogs, that is,
dogs on the Kennel Club lists as they are pedigrees, but there are
classes for the waggiest tail and the dog the judge would most
like to take home, and the brightest eyes.

They are always run for charity, and I enjoy them enormously. Janus won a cup at one and Chita has several rosettes
from them. It is a good place to enter an inexperienced dog
before showing for real.

The Open show is open to all registered pedigree dogs. In
Breed shows there are classes for every breed, and the classes
start with minor puppy, for pups over six months old, and go
right through to Open, which is for the older experienced dogs
who have won their way through the other classes, although
they do not have to have done so. If a dog wins a lower class
twice it must go up to the next class.

Only first prizes in certain classes will qualify a dog for
Cruft's. Nobody can enter that just because they want to. Puma
qualified only twice in her life for Cruft's, although she did win
many first prizes. She was there in 1974 and 1978.

Janus could not be shown in Breed as he was castrated. He

carried blindness in his pedigree; although he did not actually go blind any pups could have done. He also had very bad hips. And he was very oversexed, and I had no desire to foist faulty pups on the world knowingly or unknowingly, as he might have run off.

Everything that could go wrong with a brood bitch did go wrong with Puma, so I had Chita spayed. She can't be shown in Breed either. There are too many pups bred that nobody wants in the end, so I leave breeding to others.

Obedience shows are to see how well the dog is controlled. There are a series of exercises, all of which originally had a purpose in living with dogs. Now the top Obedience is much more like horse dressage and the standard is extremely high. It entails a great deal of training, and with huge entries you do need a very steady dog that enjoys itself performing in this way.

The classes are divided into Beginner, Novice, A, B, and C, and then Championship C. The teaching profession who regard A as the highest and C as the lowest, find this very confusing!

In the three lowest classes the dog is tested on the lead for heelwork, as well as off the lead. He must walk close to the handler, turn when the handler does, and sit when told. Owners may chat to their dogs in Beginner and Novice, but mustn't touch them, to get them to work well.

In A the only command the handler may give is 'heel'. The dog must sit when the handler stops without a command and the handler may not talk to the dog at all. This is a gradual increase in experience from the early classes, as there is still lead heeling.

The dog must be able to do correct right, left and about turns, both on and off the lead.

In Trials in the lowest stake, the Companion Dog stake (CD) the dog is also tested on the lead, but does not have to work so accurately. However the test is the equivalent of class A, not the lower classes, as the handler may not speak to the dog to encourage him.

A lot of Trials beginners fail to realise this and come in with

65

dogs that aren't up to the work as they haven't yet been trained sufficiently to drop the encouragement.

In Obedience handlers can be docked for forward sits, backward sits, crooked sits, wide working, forward working, lagging, just to name a few faults. The sit in Trials needs to be beside the handler – but nobody bothers about an inch or so either way.

The other exercises in Beginner and Novice are the retrieve and the recall, the sitstay and the downstay. In Beginner the dog may fetch his own toy and bring it back to the handler, but in Novice the dog must fetch a dumbbell, which is simply a wooden or plastic bar with two square ends, made to pick up easily.

The object is thrown, the dog runs out, picks it up, brings it back and sits in front, holding it till the steward gives the order 'Take the bell'. After this the dog must sit till the steward says 'Finish' or 'Heel your dog', and the dog has to go from the handler's front to his left side.

For the recall, handler and dog walk together across the ring; the dog sits, and is left by the handler, who walks away for the width of the ring (which is simply a number of stakes with a rope round them, of a standard size dictated by the Kennel Club rules).

The handler then calls the dog who must come fast and straight, and sit in front on command. He is then sent to heel on the steward's command.

In the stays the dog must sit for one minute, and lie down for two minutes, and not move at all during the exercise. Beginner handlers usually face their dogs; Novice handlers stand with their backs to their dogs. The Kennel Club Obedience committee have recently added a standstay to this Novice class, with the result that many of us have withdrawn from competition as we don't approve of a standstay for inexperienced dogs.

In the A class the heelwork is more difficult and lasts for a longer period; and the recall is not to sit in front of the handler but to come from behind to the heel position. This is useful as an exercise as dogs are often behind one and can be called up in this way.

The downstay is five minutes and the handler goes out of sight. Each class is a gradual sequence, taking the young dog through increasing difficulty and increasing experience up to the top. It is never wise to rush him; it doesn't work, except for the rare and lucky few.

There is also a scent exercise which in class A consists of a toy, or other non-harmful object, the dog knows well being put down among decoy toys and objects it has never seen before. He has to find his own toy, or something belonging to his handler, by its scent, which is that of his handler. This in fact can easily become a sight exercise so it must be taught carefully to avoid that. (It is being altered under new regulations.)

In B there is no heel on the lead and the heelwork is harder, with the dog tested at fast, slow and normal pace.

The dog retrieves an article, provided by the judge, which the dog has never seen before.

In the next exercise he is sent away across the ring to an area the judge has marked out, or decided upon. He must go straight, drop on command, and then after a moment or two, be called back to the handler.

The judge will bring ten identical objects (no dog uses one another dog has had). There may be ten leather strips, or ten matchboxes, or ten cigarette boxes, or ten plastic cones. The handler is given one to hold and this is then taken with tongs and put down among the others. The dog has to find out which of the ten objects was that held by his handler, and so was scented with a familiar smell.

We all smell different and the dog has a computer brain which can sort out one smell from another. We do it in a small way; we know the difference between frying onions and frying bacon.

The stays are longer at this level; there is a stand stay and in the sit and down the handlers go out of sight.

In C the heelwork is much more complex; these are top experienced dogs being tested, who have probably been working for two or more years. Again the dog retrieves the judge's article; and in the scent exercise he has to find the judge's scent on a cloth which is put down among other cloths. Two of these cloths will have decoy scents on them. I have often been scent decoy and all you do is hold the cloth while the judge holds the test cloth and put it down at the same time as the steward puts down the judge's cloth.

There is now human scent on three out of ten cloths; and the dog must work out which is the judge's scent.

The tests each carry marks. The marks are deducted from the total possible so the winner is the dog that has the lowest score, not the highest score. Two means the dog worked perfectly except for two faults; forty means the dog lost forty marks. Scent carries fifty marks so a dog failing that can lose the lot.

The tests in the lowest classes have a practical use; no one wants a dog at lead's length in a crowded street; if told to stay he must or he won't be where you left him when you come back; and it is very good for dogs to play with you and the retrieve is the happiest form of play for any dog.

We all want our dogs to come back when called every time.

Chita adores bringing her quoit to me to be thrown again and can have an enormous amount of extra exercise, as she is very energetic, without me exhausting myself.

It is especially useful when busy and to get a dog fit there is nothing better than to throw up hill, so that it has to run up hill to fetch.

A dog must qualify in a definite way before it can enter the Championship class, and try for winning that and gaining a certificate. Three Championship Certificates (CCs) under three different judges will make the dog a Champion.

One certificate entitles the owner to work at Cruft's, the year after the certificate was won. Cruft's is always in February.

Working Trials is all based on police dog work; very broadly based as few working police dog handlers enter the civilian Police Dog stake; it has different exercises to theirs.

The lowest stake is Companion Dog (CD). If you gain more than 80 per cent in every group you can put the letters CDex after your dog's name. This is the only stake you can enter at Championship level without first qualifying at an Open Trials;

80 per cent at an Open Trials enables you to enter a Championship Trials in the other stakes, but doesn't give you a title.

There are four groups of exercises in Companion Dog, all of which must be done without chatting to your dog.

The first group is the control work; with heel on the lead, heel off the lead, a recall, and a very long sendaway to nowhere. The judge will point out a distant tree and say: 'Send your dog so many yards towards that and drop him.' There are five points for heel on lead and recall and ten for sendaway and heel free – a total of thirty for the group. The minimum mark to get anywhere is 21, and you need 24 for 80 per cent.

We are often in rough fields so nobody asks for absolute accuracy, although sometimes if we are unlucky enough to have an Obedience judge we find ourselves marked far harder than any Trials judge would dream of doing. It is far from easy to find enough experienced judges these days as dog sports have suddenly become popular, and the entries now are astronomical compared with a few years ago.

The second group contains the stays: a two-minute sit with the handler out-of-sight, and a ten-minute down with the handler out-of-sight. Chita will stay for longer than that, except at Trials; and that is the exercise that usually sends us down so that we fail to qualify.

In Obedience the stays are worked out at so many points a minute. In Beginner there are 20 points in all for the downstay: one point for every six seconds, so if your dog is still for one minute you get 10 points out of the 20.

In Trials if the dog moves, even in the last second, you lose *all* the marks. At Swindon Championship Trials some years ago Chita had 79 per cent and only the downstay to do. She stood up at nine minutes and was sick as she had been whiling away her time eating grass. That was that, although we had more than enough points to qualify we had failed one complete section.

That really was frustrating!

The third exercise is the agility. Heeling, of course, is patrolling; who wants to see a police dog pulling like a steam train? And he must also do it well off lead. Retrieve is a bonding exercise, and also practises the recall to the handler in a way that has some point. Most dogs will learn to bring you something but they are a bit mystified if you call them in for nothing, and a bit miffed if you call them in and imprison them straight away on the lead when they have been having fun.

Agility consists of a three-foot clear jump (jumping a gate); a nine-foot long jump (jumping a river); and a six-foot scale (climbing a wall).

It teaches the dog to concentrate, helps to get it fit, muscles it up for active work which may be over rough country with stiles, walls and ditches, and is of general use to a serving officer. To us, of course, it seems a bit academic, but with a dog like Chita who jumps for fun and clears anything jumpable if allowed, it is a wonderful group, and she excels in it. I am a bit disappointed if we don't get 20 marks. She rarely has less than 19.

The last group is the retrieving and nosework. The dumbbell retrieve is as in Obedience, except we are often in long grass and it may turn out to be more of a search, which is perhaps why it's in the nosework section.

Then comes the search. This consists of a fifteen-yard square with three articles hidden in it. They are the size of a six-inch nail (or should be; we have had much smaller which I don't like because the dog could swallow them, and dogs have done so). The dog works alone, and the owner mustn't go in the square.

At the last search we entered Chita found a spark plug, a half beer mat and a rubber square, about 2 inches each side. She loves searching and we often get full marks for that (there are 20 in this stake – 5 for each object and 5 for style).

My pockets are always full of extraordinary objects to hide for her for practice whenever there is a chance. I beg beer mats and wine corks and small offcuts from Andrew Bennett, who makes our club dogleads. Andrew lost a leg in the Falklands war and was trained as a saddler. He makes the best saddlery I have seen for a long time and is also interested enough in what I do to save me little pieces of leather that he would otherwise throw out.

These last sections have thirty marks altogether and 21 qualifies; while 24 ensure that the dog has 80 per cent. If you can achieve an average of 80 per cent for all four sections in an Open stake, you gain a Certificate of Merit. This entitles you in UD, WD and TD to enter the Championship stake, but you can work the next stake up in Open without having qualified in the Championship Trials. This is helpful as many of us can't get to all the Trials and only do a few each year.

The next stake is Utility Dog (UD). In this the agility is the same as in Companion Dog and does not vary throughout the stakes. There is no on-lead heelwork, only off-lead, and the control work (group I) consists of heel free; sendaway, which is often one hundred yards or more away from the handler in a straight line; retrieving a dumbbell; the ten-minute downstay (this is where Chita and I come unstuck); and steadiness to the gun. The whole section has 35 marks, and 25 will qualify. If I could get full marks for everything but the stay we'd do it!

Group II in that is the agility and group III is nosework. This consists of a half-mile track, laid half an hour before the dog works. Every dog must have a track of its own to work, so that an immense amount of land is needed for this. The tracklayers are given a set pattern and each dog has the same shaped track, but of course the fields are different and some may have hazards that don't happen to others. We had a badger trail and finished up at the sett once. The track crossed the path the badger had made the night before. Chita couldn't resist that!

The track carries 95 marks and if the dog finds the article laid at the end of it, there are another 15. Chita has had 91. She has also had 35 for the track and 15 for the article which she scented on the wind. Why follow that silly path when she knew where it was? So she shot over to it, ignoring the track itself.

The search is in a twenty-five-yard square with four hidden articles and has 35 points, 7 for each article and 7 for style.

The next stake, the Working Dog (WD) differs only in having a track that is one and half hours and has two articles laid on it, and the dog must find at least one of them.

The last stake for most of us is the Tracker Dog stake (TD) in which the track is three hours old and has on it three articles of which two must be found to qualify. (Very few people go on and do the Police Dog (PD) stake, which is chase, arrest, search and quarter.)

The sendaway has a redirection on it and after the dog has gone out the required distance the handler must send him to the right or left on the judge's command.

There is a great deal of work for the dog to do; an enormous amount of very thoughtful training, and again a new and inexperienced judge with little dog knowledge can set us all back weeks by asking something as an extra gimmick that the dogs haven't been taught. Failure can upset a dog so much that it has to be coaxed back to working. They are very easily put off.

Rule one in dog training is that you never let a dog finish on failure. If you fail the track have something in your pocket to throw so the dog thinks it has succeeded, and then go away and do a baby track. It's like getting in the car again to drive after an accident; get that confidence back fast!

The police call this little track a sweetener and they always do one after the dog has had a long gruelling track for real when on duty. A short fast one with a terrific reward at the end, to eliminate the memory of that dreary day.

Though the dog may adore tracking, it is very exhausting. There are all sorts of distractions: pheasant landed there; partridge sat there; dog checks every one, and has to make itself return to the scent it is seeking. Every footstep is sniffed; imagine crawling along a half-mile road having to sniff every step someone else has taken.

It may come naturally but it is still tiring. We enjoy every second of that three-hour game of tennis, but we aren't fit for another one immediately afterwards.

Besides conditions caused by other creatures on the track (as the tracklayer can't know what has been there before or comes after), there are wind and weather conditions; conditions due to humps and hollows in the ground; or due to wind coming through badly laid hedges. I could write a book about that alone so I had better stop!

It is the most fascinating thing I know and has useful spin-offs. Friends lost two dogs on the dunes last week and tracked them with their third dog, and found them. They had run off rabbiting. I lost a key and Janus found it in long grass in a big field. Chita has found my wedding ring and my car keys. And both dogs have found no end of gloves as I am very good at losing them when walking.

I always feel that so many dogs miss out on fun and so many people don't realise what we can achieve if we try.

The trying is fun even if we get nowhere in the end.

Our dogs are far cleverer than we think.

Chapter Seven

Those who have read my other books on Chita will already know that she has a stay problem, which is odd in that it only happens in Working Trials. She does know the exercise.

Janus and Puma never failed that one, once they knew it well. Many people say, as always, it is you, not the dog, and, yes, I am prepared to believe that to some extent it might be me.

However, as always with any dog problem, it is necessary to consider a number of factors, and try to analyse just why she fails in that particular situation. It is an impossible situation as there is no way I can ever *train* her when she is being tested.

The exercise is difficult. The dog has to remain quite still, lying down, by herself for ten minutes, while the handler goes right out of sight. The dog is left in a totally new place, among total strangers and totally strange dogs. The time seems endless to the handlers. It must seem even more so to the dogs, who may well have a fear that they have now been abandoned. It takes a great deal of experience with this exercise for the dogs to feel relaxed.

Many dogs are plunged into it too soon without training. It takes a long time to get the necessary standard, building up by a minute at a time over a period of weeks, and making sure the dog *never* moves during training.

Chita in fact was very steady and she did four downstays without trouble, at Trials, after a very long initial period of considerable difficulty, as when I left her she went into a blind panic.

First of all, she is a very nervous bitch, although training has given her a good deal of security and changed that, up to a point. She still reverts under stress.

Secondly, our long association through her problems which

74

had to be overcome has made her far more attached to me than many dogs are to their owners, so that she may not be able to bear me out-of-sight without getting so stressed that she can't cope with the exercise.

There are very few people indeed who can handle her, as she simply pulls to come to me, and won't do as they tell her. So if I go, and leave her with people she feels she can play up with impunity, she gets up and comes to me.

Thirdly, she is a pack leader and very dominant indeed. The downstay is a submissive exercise, lying down among strangers, both human and canine. It means she has given up her leadership role and is now an underdog, doing as she is told, without my presence.

However, she has to learn. Also we can't read a dog's mind and I could be wrong on all counts. More people have speculated about Chita's lack of stays than about any other exercise.

There are other factors too.

At one of her earliest outings there was a sudden lightning flash just as we had all left our dogs in the stay and walked away. This was at an Obedience show where you may remain in-sight, but in this class you had to turn your back to the dog. There was the most tremendous thunder clap and every dog fled to its owner.

The judge did the stay again and allowed us to remain close to our dogs, as the circumstances were exceptional.

This incident set us back some weeks. When I felt she was steady and relaxed again I took her to another show. Here there were two rings side-by-side, sharing one rope between them. The judge in the first ring did not plan the round properly, so that when it came to throwing the wooden dumbbell, the handler had to throw towards the second ring, in which I was working Chita.

The stays are always done with all the dogs together, so that if forty compete in that class, forty dogs do the stays at the same time. This makes for very crowded rings. It is even worse when there are sixty dogs competing. The dogs are far too close and dominant dogs need a lot of space around them. Chita knows she may not attack any other dog, but it may be asking a great deal of her to remain so near to a possible threat.

She was very badly bitten when she was only sixteen weeks old, and dogs have long memories. Most dogs in Obedience today, unfortunately for her, are Collies. It has made what was once a very interesting kind of showing very stereotyped. Few of the other breeds can produce the accuracy of the Collie, so it is now being bred and bought in quantity just for competition.

I don't think this is good either for competition or for the breed. I would like to see the field widened again, to include all breeds, giving a chance to the stable, sane members of those breeds, as a good competition dog may not be the type of dog anyone would want in the family.

Some are delightful, but people who go to shows regularly know very well that some are far from being even likeable, although they may do a great deal of winning. They are dogs to avoid when you meet them out of the ring. The villain that bit Chita was a village stray, allowed to roam, but he was a Collie; and she has regarded the breed with suspicion ever since.

So that could be one factor.

At this show when it came to the stays, I sat her with her back to the centre rope of the ring, as I was trying to avoid putting her between two Collies. I walked away with my back to her and after the exercise had begun I heard Chita squeal. She ran to me, leaving a dumbbell lying where she had been sitting and an enormous German Shepherd racing to pick it up.

I thought the dumbbell had hit her. It may not have done, but even so it had landed with a thump behind her back, as she was sitting concentrating on me; the thud was followed apparently by a dog out to attack her. Small wonder she bolted.

The rules say all dogs must have exactly the same conditions. No other dog had had such a distraction. Had I been judging I would have ruled that exercise invalid owing to a major distraction and let the dog do it again, with other dogs repeating the exercise to give as close to the same conditions as possible.

The judge informed me I had better get my dog used to all hazards as you never knew what would happen at a show.

That is true, but I don't consider having a dumbbell thrown at a dog should be part of any show, even if it was an accident. The judge in the other ring was mainly to blame for not considering others when setting up the round.

At that point I decided I would give up Obedience altogether. It has ceased to be any kind of pleasure. The stay rings were far too crowded, the dogs exposed to too much stress, and it seemed a silly way to spend my time. I don't train Chita at the top of my voice and my nervous dog was being exposed to handlers bawling 'stay, stay, stay' in stentorian tones as if their dogs were deaf. It didn't really surprise me that she couldn't take it.

So now we would concentrate on Working Trials where the numbers, then, were fewer, and we were in wide open spaces with large gaps between each dog. I saw a course advertised, for dogs with problems such as stay problems and went on it.

It produced yet another hazard in a long line of misfortunes that had overtaken poor Chita in this exercise.

We left about twenty dogs spread out in a line in the field and we all walked away until we were out-of-sight. Chita had been lying relaxed and steady. Suddenly came a call of 'Handlers, return' as all hell broke loose. When I got back, a large dog had come out of line, picked on the little dog beside Chita and was shaking him like a rat, while he alternately squealed and bit. The little dog's owner tried to separate them and got bitten and the big dog's owner added to the chaos by what appeared to be hysterics.

Meanwhile Chita lay in the middle of this and I couldn't reach her.

When things did quieten down I went to her. She was shaking, she had wet herself, but she hadn't moved.

She has only done one downstay perfectly since and that was in a large field with only two other dogs, as the judge tested us in threes. Both dogs were Labradors. They were spaced very far apart and she did stay the full time. In Trials judges may test dogs one at a time if they choose, and with the numbers of

77

unsteady dogs, some with undesirable characters, that can now come into Trials, I begin to wish this was a rule.

Chita is well used to dogs. She comes into club with me and lies still while I teach. She is unleashed, by herself, and doesn't move unless I take her out for a demonstration. So it is not lack of socialisation. I think it is lack of confidence in other dogs and the people around her.

At one of her early Trials she broke her stay and unfortunately one of the stewards, who was young and inexperienced, knew her. I came back to find Chita being cuddled. That, of course, made her think that if she broke next time she would get another cuddle. She loves cuddles. Next time the steward decided she needed a lesson and told her off.

She is now wary of stewards.

There is far more to arranging a Show or Trials than just putting on something that will do. Unless judges and stewards are experienced, the results can leave much to be desired, as they can with inexperienced judges and stewards in Obedience.

I have been walked into the ring ropes, commanded to do something impossible like turn right where you can only do a left turn; had a marathon round that would sort a Cruft's competitor out, in a junior class, and at one show one judge docked me for using my voice too harshly in the first ring and an hour later I was docked by another judge for pretty, pretty handling! (I don't know what that is, but I suppose the judge did.) Neither fault is listed in the Kennel Club rules.

I have had some lovely judges but just occasionally I felt that people were out to teach Joyce Stranger some strange kind of lesson, as some of the most idiotic things did happen to me in some rings. People got to saying 'not again!'

Trials can produce inexperienced stewards and judges, but I have been much luckier there. Although we haven't qualified, I have only come away once feeling that the round was unreasonable. This was when a gimmick was introduced that meant dogs were being asked to do something they had not been trained to do. Further, the new departure was not in the regulations. All

78

the dogs failed that day, as none of them knew how to tackle the hazard that was introduced.

I rang three experienced handlers and they all said the same thing. 'Gimmicky. Make a note of the judge and don't show under that person in future.'

Competitors have the remedy in their own hands, but many perhaps don't understand that bad judging turns either an Obedience show or a Trial into a farce. The results aren't even really valid. I like showing under police dog handlers, as they are always realistic, don't bend the regulations and give you a very fair Trials indeed. I have several other favourite people who send all competitors home feeling they have failed, not because of some gimmick, but because they weren't up to what was a very fair test indeed.

We would have qualified on several occasions if only Chita had done her stay. So where could I find major distractions which wouldn't stress her unduly?

It was about this time that David Lea Wilson who is part of the Mona Sea Zoo down by the Straits, ran into problems. He had joined the club after Christmas with his young black Labrador called, of course, Haddock. What else for an Aquarium dog?

They were doing very well, but summer came. A very hot and busy summer, and David and Mark, his colleague, who owns Haddock's father, Bill, found themselves with some nineteen thousand visitors in the season. Haddock needed training. David had no time at all.

So I went down to train him, and after training Haddock trained Chita on her stays.

Haddock was used to cars coming and going, to dogs leaping out of cars, to people everywhere, to children who rushed to feed the geese and ducks and look at the now big orphan lambs, and also feed the trout. There were very free range chickens trotting round the car park.

It was one continuous bustle. As well as the Aquarium there is a craftshop, sweets are on sale and there is also a little restaurant. People seemed to come in droves. Haddock ignores

79

them completely; he is a lovely tempered dog and very easy to train. I enjoyed my sessions with him enormously.

One morning I arrived to give him his lesson and found he had gone walkabout. This isn't desirable as there are sheepfields all round the Aquarium and no farmer is happy if dogs run through his flocks, whether they chase or not.

I went to look for Haddock. 'He might be down by the Mermaid,' David said. The Mermaid Inn was about half a mile away. I drove down and parked and went on to the beach where a number of dogs were having the time of their lives, racing around, playing with one another. Among them was a young black Labrador. I called.

'Haddock.' Eyes swivelled in my direction. Everyone on the beach, which was crowded, seemed to be staring at me. I only then realised quite how absurd his name is! Luckily he broke away at once and came, so that I didn't feel quite so daft standing there apparently shouting for a fish!

He followed me to the car and I realised I hadn't really thought this one out. It is Chita's car and I was proposing to put another dog in with her. I had two chains, one each side, fastened to ringbolts, left over from the days when she and Janus travelled together. I put Haddock on one chain and Chita on the other, and drove back to the Aquarium. Luckily it wasn't far. They made faces at one another and Chita's hackles were up.

By the end of four weeks Haddock had improved enormously and Chita was used to people, everywhere, to other dogs, to chickens rushing round her, to children racing past her, and the geese. The geese weren't really sure about her. They were behind pigwire, with a small pool of water where the ducks stand and shake themselves dry and flap their wings. This intrigued Chita. She would stay, within a few inches of the wire, the geese and the ducks the other side of it, very close to her, and in constant movement and very noisy.

Children fed them, ignoring the dog. They dropped bread near her and the chickens rushed at it. I felt surely if she could stay still with this lot she could stay still at Trials.

Chita will stay for ever like this – there were seven chickens passing her – so why won't she stay at Trials?

Janus: the last picture we have of him, taken a few months before he died.

Getting to know each other: Chita's greeting to new dog Josse isn't particularly friendly.

Above A daily sight from our dining room window at breakfast time, across the river and up the hill.

Left Teaching Haddock the sit stay.

Two kinds of showing;
Above The judge at a
Breed show goes over
the little dog on the
table to assess its points
and soundness.

Left Children parade
their dogs at a Pet
show.

It takes imagination to beat the weather sometimes! Anne Malcolm Bentzen's Samoyed Sailor dressed for the rain, and wearing the new halter which stops him pulling without cutting his fur as a choke would.

Barbara Swain Williams's latest acquisition, Hugo, was feeling the heat, even under his sunshade.

Let's not bother to compete today: it's much more fun watching all the other dogs!

Weaving lesson on one of 1985's rare fine summer evenings.

Although old and quite deaf, Janus still enjoyed outings in the car with Chita.

Posing for the camera always starts this way: it takes time to convince Chita that Seán does not want to play. She also thinks the light meter is edible.

Left Chita gains full marks over the hurdle.

Below Eric Roberts sending Fons off on a long sendaway. The sendaway can be boring for the dog, but Eric's immense enthusiasm brings out enthusiasm in his pupils, whether canine or human.

On one occasion Chita was on a downstay by the goose pen when somebody suddenly hurled a ball towards her. It hit the fence about two feet away from her, followed by Haddock, hurtling after it. I was ready with a command, but she didn't need it. To my delight, she stayed through what was a very major distraction, as she loves balls and does not love other dogs flying towards her at speed.

During the sessions Seán Hagerty wanted to take photographs for *A Dog in a Million*. He came down to the Aquarium and photographed Chita on her stay. She adores Seán, perhaps more so as he is bearded and she has a passion for bearded men. I always hope my judges won't be bearded as she can't take her eyes off them.

She always poses beautifully for the camera, as if she were aware that Seán wants her cooperation. She loves playing to the gallery and shows off. There she was, head held regally, eyes on Seán, her attitude saying 'Aren't I good? Aren't I beautiful?' when a gander, annoyed by her presence near to a piece of bread, hurtled over and pecked her on the rump.

She turned and snapped at him, but didn't move, and Seán was quick enough to photograph her as she did so. That session ended there, as her expression of indignation was so funny we couldn't stop laughing. Chita knew she was the star turn, so was that why she stayed?

I have yet to find out. Our first Working Trial of the year is some weeks away. Have all those sessions paid off, or is a Trial something different?

All I can do is practise all the time and wait and see.

Chapter Eight

There are so many kinds of dog days. I don't often judge, as I haven't really wanted to waste time that I might have spent in training and competing with my own dog. Time is so scarce and so precious.

I have judged four times, at very small shows, which are usually much more fun as there is no pressure on anyone to want to win an award that is going to qualify them to work in a higher class.

The first show I ever judged was a Responsible Owners' Show at Cardiff. Janet Martineau, who is one of the top competitors in her part of the country and who writes the Obedience column in *Our Dogs*, came as my steward and I stayed with her before and after the show, at her Gloucestershire home.

Owners were not experienced. They had already done a written test which we had to mark and now had to do a practical test. I had them walk round the ring, ask the dogs to sit, down and stand, and meet my dog and behave when they met it.

Janus was my test dog. He could usually be relied on to behave himself, but he had one or two pet hates and did have to be watched.

Most of the dogs were well behaved but we had trouble with one little Terrier. He was an absolute imp of mischief. He escaped from his owner and chased a goat, as it was that sort of pet show. I did not know how on earth to mark his heelwork. Did I take off a point for every chair he cocked his leg against, or count it as one fault? Whatever I did, he had very few points left.

I was reminded of him last session at our club tests when the owner of one of our most mischievous little dogs, a delightful Westie, suddenly said, as he shot round the room instead of walking at her heels: 'Please God, don't let him cock his leg!'

God must have heard her as he didn't.

Marian, who came some years ago with her dog Rags, used to say of an owner whose dog did misbehave during his first lesson: 'Joyce, shall I go and comfort them and tell them about Rags?'

Rags was a RSPCA rescue dog, of a hundred different varieties, all rather badly mixed, and he had electrified us on his first night in club by cocking his leg against the table, five chairs and three pianos that for some reason graced our hall. He blotted his copybook when being road and car tested by cocking his leg in the judge's car. Rags was incorrigible, but I once caught him in midstream and flapped my hand across his back and said 'NO' at the top of my voice and he was so shocked he never did it again in club.

I had no emergency kitchen roll with me when judging this naughty little dog who seemed to need to mark every chair.

When judging in Obedience you start with one hundred points and deduct a mark for every mistake. Joey made about a thousand mistakes. Janet and I dared not look at one another as it was hard not to laugh and his poor owner was so desperate. He was such an awful little dog. But he did have the most soulful eyes.

For the rest of the day every time we heard a dog bark we said 'Bet that's Joey,' and it was.

I have judged two local shows here. It is never easy to judge a Pet Show, as the classes can be odd. How do you judge a tortoise against a goldfish? The most talkative budgerigar class always turns out to have an entry so embarrassed not one will open its beak and sing. At the first of the two Pet Shows one of the rabbits managed to get into a cage with another rabbit in it, by some very odd procedure on its part, and we had a feeling the worst had happened.

I always want to give prizes to everyone! They all love their pets and it's so hard to have to pick out just three from thirty and say these are the best. My winner of the best dog was a Collie that proved to be well over ten years old and was in the most beautiful condition. I said I had picked the oldest dog in the best condition and owners kept coming to me with even older dogs that weren't in nearly such good condition and grumbling because theirs hadn't been chosen.

There were only two ponies in the horse class. One was a charming elderly fellow aged twenty-six and the other a beautiful little Welsh Mountain pony of only six years old. How on earth could I judge them one against the other? In the end I asked if we couldn't make it two classes; one for the oldest and one for the youngest so both owners went home happy. The old fellow was wonderful, but compared against a youngster he had had his day.

I picked out my best rabbit, and somebody came up and informed me it was in too good a condition and would be dead within three weeks. A whisper told me that this was another rabbit owner, so I ignored that and gave the rosette to a lively happy black and white imp with bright eyes and a shining coat and a great deal of energy.

The tortoises defeated me completely. How on earth do you judge four shells? They were all unionised and on strike. So the prize in that class went to the only goldfish, which was at least moving and in tip-top condition. I still don't understand how they arrived at that group. Pets that didn't come into any other category?

Then came the most obedient dog. I decided that the sixty dogs would all do a sitstay. I eliminated dogs that were held up, or propped up, and evicted the boy whose dog started five fights, and had to be stopped every time, and then had an elimination contest. As few people knew what obedience meant, that proved excessively difficult and my winner was regarded as unfair as he had been to classes and nobody else had. But a dog that does as it's told was the object of the exercise and how on earth could it be judged otherwise?

The cats ought to have been easier. Somebody had brought a mother cat with four blind kittens. I wasn't aware of them until I saw a girl of about twelve standing by them, heaving. 'I've never seen anything so disgusting in my life,' she said, and her mother agreed. 'How dare they bring that here?'

The other children were enchanted, watching her suckle her tiny mewing young and wash them, totally absorbed by her little family and quite unworried by spectators. She was in a large cage, in her bed. 'I thought they'd like to see it,' the owner explained. I didn't think it very wise as there could have been infection about, but it was a pretty basket full of proud motherhood and all but the poor child who had had no proper education about animals were delighted at the thought.

One little girl came to me a moment later with an empty box containing a pad of pink cottonwool.

'It had a gerbil in it,' she said. 'It had babies at dinner time and mummy wouldn't let me bring it but I brought you the box to show I really do have a gerbil.'

Children's logic can be defeating at times! I managed not to laugh and congratulated her on the family and then went to find the biggest cat.

This was very easy as there, sitting in a patch of sunlight, was the most immense cat I had ever seen. He lay on the lap of an extremely old man who looked at me rather blankly. I handed him the rosette for the largest cat.

'What's this?'

'It's for the biggest cat.'

'He's a very big cat,' he said and handed me back the rosette. This happened about five times, and in the end I pinned it on him and said 'It's for you.'

'He's a very big cat,' he said.

The smallest cat was equally easy; a midget Siamese that I longed to take home. The prettiest kitten was impossible and I ended up doing a mental eeny-meeny-miny-mo.

Best in Show was equally impossible. I knew that whatever I did would find disfavour with practically everybody but the winner, and I don't remember now how I did solve that one. At that point I made a mental note that judging wasn't all it was cracked up to be.

Then came the last class of all, and now I was sure that the show organisers had determined that the judge would go home so unpopular that she would never ever be asked to judge again. I had to find the nicest owner in the show!

The prize, I decided, would go to the youngest owner. We asked for the youngest there and up came eight five year olds!

So then I knew it had to go to the oldest owner there, and I took the big rosette to the old man and his cat.

'What's that for?' he asked.

I told him.

'He's a very big cat,' he said. I pinned on the rosette and he looked even more bewildered. I wondered if Grandad had been brought for the afternoon to sit somewhere warm among people, and had no idea what he was really doing there, in the big hall, holding his cat. He seemed as mystified as the cat must have been.

I went home wondering if any of the competitors would ever speak to me again. I had a phone call that night. Five of the prizes I had given had all been won by various members of the same family, which had apparently caused a near riot after I had left.

I didn't know any of them and I had certainly not realised it as no surnames were used, only Christian names. What I did know was that that family most certainly did know how to keep all their pets in magnificent condition.

The second pet show was very similar to the first and quite as difficult to judge. The only thing I could go for was the best condition as I am not up in the finer points of rabbits, hamsters, gerbils, tortoises, budgerigars and parrots. I tend to be odd in that I regard a dog or cat in top condition as a better specimen than the one that is just like the breed standard but is appallingly unfit.

The last show I judged was a little Exemption show in the Midlands. It was a long drive, added to by the fact that I had to collect my steward who lives over thirty miles away from me in the wrong direction. That added sixty miles to an already long journey.

We arrived to find we were to judge in rings that were staked out on a partially flooded set of tennis courts. This added to the fun. It was a cold day and we arrived starving to find that there were two parts to the show, Breed and Obedience, and they were apparently at war.

We were told judges and stewards were to be given some food and a hot drink by the Breed people. They were so refined they apparently didn't have appetites at all. We were rather crude and were ready to eat a horse each. We were given one half-sandwich each and a tepid brew that might have been tea, coffee, cocoa or Bovril. It did nothing to alleviate our hunger pangs, and we had all day to judge. We had stopped for coffee and a slice of toast en route and were very thankful we had.

I was judging two classes: one all German Shepherds at Beginner standard and the other all gundogs. It was a lovely day and I enjoyed every moment of it, apart from ending up so hungry that we were desperate and went to find the Obedience show manager who was appalled to hear we had been fed on tiny elegant bits of food that wouldn't keep the wolf from the door and were hungry enough to eat the tennis nets. They provided soup and a quiche and we fed voraciously and even then stopped on the way home to eat a large meal, as I was sure I would never manage the last sixty miles suffering from hunger pangs all the time.

Food is very important when you are judging or stewarding as you have to concentrate so hard. Competing means standing around in the cold all day very often, or the rain, or a howling gale. You get very hungry. Food has often been one of the problems for competitors at many shows. You ring the secretary before a Trials. Will food be available? Oh yes, and when you arrive you find it's not.

If you put up in a pub overnight they may not give you sandwiches and never give you flasks of soup.

At one Trial, in mid March when it was blowing a gale and snowing, I discovered they were serving meals in an annexe to the main room and went in and asked for mine and paid for it. At the end one of the helpers came up and said 'Which stake are you judging?' 'None of them. I'm competing.' 'Oh, Lord. The food was only for the judges!' It was too late by then. I'd eaten it!

Or they have to put the catering out to franchise otherwise they don't get the venue and the caterers provide a cooked meal of fish and chips or pie and chips and you arrive late, having had to work late and discover all you can have is soggy chips.

A pub meal can be good; it can be, as one was, last year, an overcooked microwaved potato with bullet hard baked beans served with a snarl. Another pub kept us waiting an hour in pouring rain, determined not to open till 1 p.m. We had always thought pub hours were earlier, but that pub was a law unto itself. The landlord added insult to injury by watching us through a window and the food when it came wasn't worth having.

All in all, many of these organisers ought to come with me to Worthing and have a lesson from those who run Findon Downs annual Obedience Show, which is quite one of the best I have ever attended. Especially their food. That would larn them!

Chapter Nine

It is, unbelievably, eighteen years since the letter from Findon Downs Dog Training Club landed on my door mat. I never dreamed where it was to lead me in the distant future!

I was still borrowing dogs, I was writing, I was chairman of a group of the Books for Your Children, which was far from an easy task as I had a very odd committee. My committees nearly always do seem a bit odd; they have such wonderful unrealistic ideas, especially when it comes to money. Everyone in the world they know is longing, they are sure, to give their services free. People in *my* world need paying, as they can't subsidise every club in existence and spend their time talking for nothing. Travel and keep cost cash.

One of my committee meetings started with me saying: 'We talk about books for your children. We do not provide *free* books. We can't expect speakers to come free either.'

Unfortunately in these days when petrol costs almost £2 a gallon and time is increasingly precious, travelling and speaking for nothing is a luxury few of us can afford.

My fees in the early days varied from a posy of flowers from someone's garden, or a tablet of fancy soap, to a mere thanks, if anyone actually remembered. Often they didn't and I went out wondering why on earth I had travelled, dressed up, rehearsed and come. I was talking to WIs and other women's groups, who use up speakers in quantity all over the country, to luncheon groups, which was often hell as they didn't really want *me*, they just wanted an entertainer, and I am not that.

I often sat and ate in solemn silence as nobody knew quite what to make of me! One waitress at one function came over and said: 'You can't sit there. That's for the speaker.' I drew myself up to my five foot one inch as best I could and said: 'I *am* the speaker.' She stared at me, as I plainly wasn't at all what a speaker ought to look like. What ought a speaker to look like? Large, portly, impressive and draped in diamonds? I just don't know!

I made up my mind that I wasn't going to speak to any political group any more. I would still go to schools; they are fun and the children are rewarding, mostly. One or two schools remain memorable as horror stories, especially one which I went to during a teachers' strike.

I will in future also strike during a teachers' strike as I have no intention whatever of being exposed to a rabble of yahoos, as I was that day. The young males of the human species especially resembled nothing more than a group of very unpleasant apes. In fact I prefer apes, as they don't know any better.

Speak to a dog club? Now that was different. Having my own dog was only a short way away as I knew Kym had cancer and not so long to live. The family weren't aware of it, yet, but when Kym died I would have my own dog. I was tired of not having a dog. I was tired of having Publicity ring me and going off at a moment's notice to Ireland or Edinburgh or some country town where I slept in a commercial hotel (in those days only my paperback publishers paid expenses) surrounded by bawdy half-drunk reps and my bed had sheets with holes in them and the water from nextdoor's wash basin came up into mine when he went to bed, and somebody was always noisily sick.

Publicity events always seem to be arranged at a moment's notice and you are supposed to rush and do them with your tongue hanging out in gratitude. If you are very lucky somebody might actually come and buy your book. When you write a book they keep it for months and when they edit it they keep it for months and then you get it back to work on at top speed, which isn't always convenient. But authors aren't meant to eat or have lives of their own, I decided long ago.

If they had to eat they might get more respect from their readers who never buy them but borrow them at 0.92p a time, which they don't even pay. The Government does!

Actually my publishers and readers aren't like that these

days, but fourteen years ago I had a different publisher and I felt I was merely slave labour, working for peanuts and speaking for free.

I wanted a dog, but a dog didn't fit in with that kind of life. Who looked after it while I lived it up in some ghastly commercial hotel? If I had a dog I had a good excuse not to do all those strange things that felt like jumping through hoops most of the time. If I had a dog I would be able to relax again, to walk again when I chose, and not when it was convenient for my borrowed dog's owner, to go back to the country life I loved that was being overlaid by city affairs that prevented me from gaining new experiences for writing.

One of the most frightening functions I have ever attended was to speak at a luncheon to coincide with the publication of one of my books. I prepared a flippant little speech on being a writer, and then, when we arrived I was horrified to find about ten other authors there, all far better known than I was, among them John Braine and, I think, Melvyn Bragg.

The speech I had prepared just wouldn't go down in such company. I cursed the publicity manager inwardly for not warning me; it was a very daunting audience for a new author. My appetite vanished. I sat, being careful not to touch any wine as I needed all the wits I had. (I don't like drinking in the middle of the day and drink very little at the best of times.) I was racking my brains. What the dickens *was* I going to talk about?

I finally talked about the way I research my books. About events such as hiding behind a tractor with a photographer while the farmer and his hands try to pen a rampaging bull using pitchforks; standing helpless, idiotically wearing a skirt, in the cage of a baby orang-utan that put her hand up my skirt, discovered my pants and began to pull at them! The men around me were convulsed with laughter, the baby had the hardest and strongest hands I had ever met and I stood there hanging on to my dignity for all I was worth, as they struggled to remove her. I never wore skirts on an assignment again.

There was also the time we were roped in, because we knew about the ways of sheep, to act as sheepdog when they were

91

dipping sheep, on the way back from the beach on a scorching summer day, dressed in our bathing costumes. The farmer's brother had forgotten they were dipping and gone off to their other farm with all the dogs. Softly softly, herdee sheepee.

Once we had them then there was the wild struggle to convince them they actually wanted to be drowned, as they were sure that was what we were after. Splashing bodies thrashing in the dip, dip all over us, lambs who weren't being dipped yelling for their mothers, except for two ram lambs who followed Mum up the ramp and stood on her head, and nearly did succeed in drowning her.

I've a feeling it was John Braine who commented: 'My research isn't a bit like that.'

Certainly I couldn't imagine any of them sitting in a tree watching foxcubs play; or hiding at dawn to see the badger cubs come out; or following the stalker down the forest to see if we could spot the new deer babies, or lying on the moors at a loch-side watching osprey fish.

How can you convey to city people the utter excitement of having a newly tamed foxcub feeding from your hand; or a little badger cub coming to you and musking your shoe, laying his claim to you as a friend, the wild mite full of trust. The pheasant that comes for food; the walk through the pen where the rabbits and pheasants live together, and the dogs ignore them; the pleasure of seeing the ferret coming out of his straw to greet you, delighted to have company again.

These to me are the realities, and they will still be there long after Man is only a sad and foolish memory, exterminated by his own curiosity and rapacity.

I needed to be out in the fields, down by the river, or walking under the trees.

I was tired of borrowing Max or Kirsty or Heidi or Bill or Sandy. I was tired of being envious of people who mostly didn't seem to even want their dogs at all.

I realised how stupid I was being the day that someone rang me and said: 'Can you come and talk on such-and-such a date? I do hope you can as you're the fifth person we've asked.'

I promptly said no and rang off. First choice, I might have gone. Fifth choice? They had to be joking!

Findon Downs Dog Club looked like being the first audience I had had of people who might understand my world. They were all dog owners.

(I hadn't realised then that there were dog clubs. I knew about Breed shows as our nextdoor neighbours showed their two English Setters. I knew nothing about Obedience or Working Trials.)

My aunts lived in Worthing and this was only a couple of miles away. I could go down, visit my parents in Bexhill and stay with my two aunts, then in their late seventies, and I didn't mind if there was no fee as the aunts were poppets and I was very fond of them.

I wrote back and said yes. I was invited as I was staying in the area to come to the club and see the dogs perform. I went to club and was very impressed by their mass downstays; about twenty dogs on the floor, owners off the floor; no dogs moving. I could teach a dog to stay, but I had never tried that sort of training, en masse. When I got my dog I would go to a dog club.

I spoke for half the evening. The other part was occupied by a film about Guide Dogs. My aunts were invited too and to their delight had VIP chairs in the middle of the front row and at half-time a tray each laid with a pretty cloth and with someone's best china, sandwiches and scones and a little posy of flowers. It made their evening for them, and they often spoke of it afterwards as they led very secluded lives now both were retired.

That night I met Doris Strotten, who had written to me and who was the club instructor, and Fred Herman, whose future was as yet unwritten. At that time he owned a Labrador named Sandy and had not yet become hooked on Obedience shows. I met Sandy and the Corgi Rufus and Fred's wife Doris. I didn't know that in the audience was someone who was to become part of my life later on.

A few months later I was invited to become one of Findon Downs' vice-presidents. I accepted and offered to give them a

93

shield. This was the Rex Award and I was to personally present it to the winner, and, for some reason I can't remember, *Woman's Realm*, who were maybe serialising Rex, were to photograph me doing so at the summer dog show, which was, I believe, the first they ever had.

I dressed up for the occasion. Nobody told me that dog shows of this sort aren't garden party occasions. You go in trousers and anoraks; and wear woolly hats. They are far from elegant and even in summer can be very cold. That day there was a strong wind off the sea and I *was* very cold. There was I, all dolled up, feeling an utter idiot, in a two-piece green outfit with a summery hat that wouldn't stay on, wearing high-heeled shoes, which I never wear, feeling as out of place as a goldfish in a tank of sticklebacks.

The photograph was terrible and the magazine very kindly didn't publish one with me in it. The shield was won by a Sheltie and she and her owner made a nice picture. I was sent the photograph in which I featured in all my ridiculous finery and still have it as a momento of an occasion that went badly wrong.

After I became a vice-president of the Findon Downs Club I always planned my annual visit to my parents in June and then was able to take Janus and Puma to their show. I always stayed with my two aunts who were now aging fast.

During those years Fred Herman bought another dog, a Border Collie named Moss. Moss won Cruft's Obedience in 1974. Fred left the club and started a competition club of his own and two people who were soon to become good friends of mine took over the club to prevent it folding. It is always very difficult to keep dog clubs going as it is so hard to find people willing to give their time to helping, and also people capable of instructing competently.

Anne Malcolm Bentzen became secretary and Pat O'Shea became Treasurer. Anne owned a lovely Samoyed named Bosun and Pat had a cross-bred dog named Butch that had started life as a vicious rescue dog and when I knew him was a sweet and sensible animal.

One of my favourite photographs is of Butch, Bosun, Janus,

94

Puma and Chita sitting in a line outside the house in Rustington, which they left some years ago. Only Chita is still alive.

Somehow, over the years, we have come to share so many memories, although we meet rarely, phone only occasionally and live over three hundred miles apart.

Chapter Ten

People rarely realise how much their lives with their dogs are influenced by the place in which they live. Eric Roberts has, at present, under his care, a Bull Mastiff. The dog has only one idea in its head and that is to kill stock.

It is a beautiful friendly animal, very safe with people. It belonged in a family, but the dog is so powerful and so black determined to get at other animals that they could not control it. It was sent to Eric for training. He gave it a three-week course and when it went home its obedience was perfect, but the sight of other animals sent it berserk. Sadly, the owners asked Eric to find the dog a new home. They loved their dog well enough to know that if they kept him he would transgress so badly that he would have to be destroyed. They simply lived in the wrong environment for him.

The search for the ideal home has been extremely difficult and the dog is still at the kennels, long past the time which was sensible to keep him, but Eric, like so many of us, cannot bear to say goodbye to a young dog. He will not sell him to a family, nor to anyone who lives within reach of stock, so his choice is very limited. The right kind of home needs to have a ten-foot wall round it and no chance whatever of the dog ever being able to get near farm animals.

It is not always possible to find out whether dogs are safe with stock. When Janus and Puma were young we lived in a town and our walks were either round the roads, so at least they were well used to traffic, or in the park, where an enterprising and imaginative council had bought five acres of fields for dogs and children to roam in, unhindered. There were streams to dam and trees to climb. There was long grass where dogs could run free.

Yet oddly, we had the park almost for our own exclusive use. The only wildlife, apart from birds, were squirrels and rabbits, and the aftermath of a fox. We never saw him, but he left his trail.

It was very different when we moved here. In 1976 Janus was five and Puma was four: both young, both energetic and both unused to country roads with no pavements and to fields containing sheep or cattle.

Our house then was far from ideal. The bathroom was rudimentary, a lean-to containing a suite so old it might have qualified for a museum. The cottage roof was slate, old and mossy and leaky and in bad repair. All the walls needed to be stripped back to the brickwork or stonework and replastered. There were years of work before we could breathe a deep sigh, say goodbye to the builders and call it home.

The two-acre grounds, which are mostly wild paddock still, were unfenced. There were sheep nextdoor and there were pigs on the other side. We grew used to waking to find a remarkably bad-tempered sow and her large son wandering in our garden. We never grew used to the fact that Janus loved to roll in their droppings; pig droppings are the same colour as a Golden Retriever. He then rolled on our carpet, which was more or less the same colour as he was.

The only thing to do was to hose him down and to clean the carpet. Copious quantities of air freshener were needed; open windows, whatever the weather; and Janus himself, after being dried, was dusted with my talcum powder to disguise the clinging smell. Puma used to go over and sniff him with an air of total disgust, more, I am sure, due to the perfume than the aftermath of pig.

Kenneth, who is less used to farmstock than I, suggested that I herded the pigs home. Instead the sow tried to herd me home, very forcefully, and she was enormous. I had no desire to be crushed. After that we left them the garden, put the dogs on the lead and walked them elsewhere. The pigs always went home at feeding time, but our garden seemed to hold better food value than their own grounds nextdoor or across the river. We were never sure who owned them as nobody admitted it!

It was a great relief when at last the men came to do the fencing and we were secure, although I still shudder when I remember the size of the bill. It cost nearly £1,000, and that was in 1976. Heaven knows how much it would cost now.

Even so it wasn't entirely sheep-proof. There were cattle in the field nextdoor and a thick hawthorn hedge between, so we did not fence that side. Then our neighbours moved the cattle and put in sheep. I was sure the hedge was not sheep-proof but they assured me it was.

I was right.

Next morning I took Puma out, luckily on the lead as by then she was blind and became agitated if she lost touch with me, and there in our garden were eleven sheep and lambs. The wind was blowing from us to them, so Puma didn't scent them. I put her indoors, hurriedly, and tried to herd the sheep into their own field but the gap they had made was enormous. In no time at all they were back.

Their owners came and herded them into their own field and blocked the hedge, but the sheep were determined and our grass was much longer, as it is not grazed. Back they all came again and there was I, with a large field of our own, having to exercise my two dogs on the lead.

I asked the farmer if he could do something about the hedge, as I do try to keep my dogs out of his flock. He was back that afternoon with fence posts and pigwire and he and his men worked right into the night, using the tractor's headlights. By morning the field was secure and I have never had sheep through since. It is a pity all farmers aren't like that. We have always been very lucky with our neighbours here.

After that both dogs were walked, as often as possible, past fields in which were bullocks, or sheep, or horses, to get them so used to the smell of the animals that they did not pull towards them. By the time we had lived here for a year, they were able to ignore even running sheep, but I never took them into a sheepfield and I took care to try and avoid lanes where I knew sheep were liable to break through and run along the road.

When Chita was sixteen weeks old I went out with the mountain rescue team on an assessment day. It proved extremely interesting as among the tests was a sheep test. The dog under test had to lie still in the middle of a field. The farmer, the handler and a spare dog were at the hedge. A flock of sheep were then driven in fast through a gate, across the field, past the dog, out through another gate and then back again.

The extra dog was to race out and intercept any dog that tried to chase the sheep, but he was not needed. Twelve dogs were tested, none of them sheepdogs, and all passed what is an extremely gruelling test of any dog. Chita watched with interest but sat still, which was surprising as she is still a very hyperactive animal now at eight years old and as a puppy was incredible. In the end she curled up and went to sleep, as we stood with the farmer and handler at the edge of the field, while sheep were driven past her not once but twenty-four times.

I would still never trust Chita free with sheep, but recently Liz Roberts and I were training at Callanway and put our dogs on a downstay and went some distance away from them. Quite suddenly two ewes and a lamb came running over the hill. Neither Sheena nor Chita moved. Chita has also run in a field where there are goats and not tried to chase.

After the sheep tests we went out, in rather bad weather (it was February), to watch dogs searching. They search a large area, scenting on the wind, to find victims, in this case Youth Hostellers taking the part of lost climbers. People suffering from exposure may crawl into strange places, such as rock crevices or under trees that have fallen, so the dog has an arduous task.

Mountain rescue dogs must also be taught to refrain from licking bloodstained clothing or bleeding wounds – many climbers who fall suffer from head injuries. So the dog is taught to search and find rags soaked in pig's blood, and to bark but not to sniff or lick.

The dogs wear plastic jackets with a light attached as often they are searching in appalling weather conditions and/or at night. The jacket is very strong and reenforced, so that they can be attached to the winch of a helicopter and lifted out of danger, or put down in a difficult area to search without first exhausting themselves by having to climb to it. Few accidents happen in easy terrain. The dogs grow accustomed to this surprisingly fast. Recently I was working with dogs where there were a number of helicopters, some being tested, others being manoeuvred. The dogs took very little notice indeed.

Every branch of dog training is different. A police dog tracks scent left on the ground by a walking or running man. A mountain rescue dog cannot do this as his territory is different. Also there may be no track; someone may simply have fallen over a precipice. So the dog searches for human scent borne on the wind.

Control of these dogs or of a police dog that may have to arrest a criminal one minute or find a lost child or old person suffering from amnesia the next, must be absolute. Yet responsibility must be left with the dog.

The Guide Dog has to take full responsibility. He has to be taught to cross the road safely; to find the bank, the chemist, the railway station; to guide his owner through narrow doorways, perhaps with the owner carrying a suitcase; to avoid obstacles and negotiate roadworks or narrow places; and one dog regularly took his owner over a catwalk high up on a multistorey building.

Much of the work is difficult to teach, in almost any field of dog training. A recent television programme showed a novice trainer taking a sheepdog into Trials; he did extremely well, but nobody can learn to control a dog in a few short weeks.

The police dog course is thirteen weeks of hard training, but at the end of it the dog is still a novice dog and inexperienced. Only time can cure that. Dogs live such a short while and just as you achieve your goal with your dog, he dies; and you start again with a new youngster with all about life yet to learn, and a lot of growing up to do.

The police dog is not trained to go out to any object, or to find game, but to a point on a field with nothing on the ground to attract him. If a thief runs through a gate and then along a wall and there is a gap in the wall, the dog can be sent to the gap to cut him off and detain him until the policeman comes. This is far more demanding of the dog than a gundog running out after shot birds.

There is a tremendous instinctive drive to run after game of any sort, and though the dog has to be restrained from tearing his trophy apart and eating it, which admittedly takes skill, there is an incentive to go out. There is no incentive whatever at first to run to a gap in a wall.

In the same way the sheepdog's instinct is to chase and kill sheep. This has to be held in control and the training is based on the channelling of an instinct. All dog training, done well, utilises the dog's natural desire. The track is based on his urge to hunt for food. That is no longer necessary, so he is trained to hunt on human scent, and find a human at the end of a track.

Wherever a driving need can be utilised, training is easy.

There is little or no skill needed to teach a gundog to retrieve. The desire is there, often so strong that it can be seen at seven or eight weeks, and a puppy can be selected on its ability at that age. The Guide Dog people, who often use Labradors, or Labrador/Golden Retriever crosses, also select pups on that basis as a pup that retrieves and brings its trophy back is intelligent. I doubt if anyone would select a Terrier on that criterion but many Terriers will retrieve.

I recently watched a little Labrador bitch do her first retrieve ever. She only had to be shown the dummy and her head went up. I know all about that, her eyes said, and she flew out and brought it back.

That can be worked on and improved and the dog brought to a high standard, but the trainer is starting with what is already there. Anyone teaching a non-retriever to retrieve, is actually working on something that is not there and will need to use skill and cunning to achieve a result.

Many dogs that come to club have long ago lost all the drives that characterised their breed. They have been bred for show-ing, which breeds for shape and conformation to an ideal picture of the dog. Some breeders now of the guard dogs are going in for Working Trials, so that the working instinct is being

101

brought back by a small band of very knowledgeable folk; in the same way there are gundog breeders who enter field trials with their dogs.

But in the main the show dogs have lost their instinctive drives, and the result is that the owners have to work exceedingly hard, even with the gundog breeds, to persuade them that retrieving is fun.

With the bull breeds that have been bred to fight there is not only the need to civilise the dog, but, in throwbacks, which do occur, to remove by training an instinct so strong that even training to a high degree of control may never eradicate it. The urge is there, just as the sexual urge is there, and few dogs driven by that will work well. There is a story of six police dogs in one force looking for an escaped prisoner. They all converged on one house. In which was a bitch in season!

I don't know if the story is true or not but it could well be. Janus was always impossible to work at combined Breed and Obedience shows as for some unknown reason it is permissible to take bitches on heat to Breed shows. He worked with his nose in the air, looking like the Bisto kid. 'I know that smell. Let me go. Better things to do than prance round a show ring doing heelwork.'

One of the saddest stories I was told was of a mountain rescue dog that had been working for three years on the hills and found his accident victims very successfully. One day, running over a hollow, a ewe stood up. He bit through her jugular, killing her, and ran on to find the object of his search. That was the end of his career. He could never be trusted again. An age-old instinct had surfaced in a moment of stress, and he had given way to it.

The worst dog of all is a Collie gone rotten. He has all his skill and can hunt down his quarry and, instead of remembering the training he has had, he kills. So many of us forget that our dogs, if dumped in the wild, would revert within days to hunters and kill rabbits and rats and mice in order to survive.

We overlay their instincts. We can never completely eradicate them if they are bred in either deliberately or by throwback.

102

Chapter Eleven

Chita has never lived in a town, but it is easier to transfer a dog from country to town than vice versa. Admittedly towns are noisy and full of people, but she has walked in towns, she comes to the hairdresser with me, she can walk through the Bangor streets.

Changing suddenly to fields full of stock and wide open spaces is heady for a dog and many a town dog comes to grief when it first meets sheep. Chita also is used to cats. She meets the vets' four cats quite often, as I call in for vitamin pills and for her panteric tablets as she has a very slight pancreas deficiency. She only needs one tablet a day, but she does need that tablet.

There is a fifth cat at the surgery now, as they rescued a small stray. It was very far from fit and was being treated and fed up before it was found a new home. Somehow this tiny cat stayed on and became one of the practice cats. It is a small charmer, and though probably a year old is very undersized as it had never been fed properly.

All these cats are used to dogs and Chita ignores them. She and Chia, our Siamese, now a very elderly lady of fourteen and solemn and staid, live happily together. If there is a strange cat on our field and Chita is running free, then, unless I see it first, she is off. It is not just cat; it is an intruder.

It is difficult for some of my town friends who have not visited to understand our problems here. The dogs see no one; there is no paper delivered. It goes to Liz, who brings it down when she comes to work as she housekeeps for me.

The post is left in the mailbox by the gate which is over two hundred yards from the house. We never see the postmen. If they do need to come down with registered mail or a heavy Christmas delivery, then they sit in the van and hoot, in case the dogs run at them. Chita is very apt to tell unknown people just where they get off!

We are so remote that we cannot see another house in summer when the leaves are on the trees. Our lane is a narrow cart track, grassy in the middle, just one car wide. Nothing bigger than a Ford pickup can get down it. There is no milk delivery. I buy longlife milk once a month.

No one ever calls casually; no one except the Lifeboat lady and the Red Cross lady ever calls for subscriptions. Days can pass with no one but Liz coming down the lane. All our family live away from us: Anne in Lymm, Andrew in Macclesfield, Nick in Barnsley, so that their visits are rare. The dogs simply don't see people. I have to go out and find people, or they might not like people at all. So I take them to various places every afternoon.

It is easy to stop dogs barking when folk call if they call often, but when they come rarely it is far less easy. Again, so much with dogs depends on where you live and how you live. My dogs are with me continuously. Kenneth is busy and though he used to take Janus out, never takes Chita as she won't even walk with him. She pulls to come to me, as she does with almost anyone who takes her. Eric said when I asked him once to take her, 'She'll make me look a fool,' and it is only recently, knowing her better, that he has taken her and worked her a little, but I have to go out of sight. He has only done it twice. I prefer to train my own dog to having it trained. That would give me little satisfaction.

Going over to Eric, I often discussed the chance of taking on another pup rather wistfully; Chita would probably not take to a pup and would be so bossy with it it would never be happy.

Anglesey is so far from everywhere that when I go to Shows or Trials it is a three-day affair; put up with friends if I can; or in a hotel if I can't, and that gets more and more expensive as prices rise every year. The cost of petrol and overnight stays is so astronomical that it is better not to work it out.

Had we remained near Manchester life would have been very different. There are shows there within a fifty-mile radius almost every week; there are Trials in Yorkshire and Staffordshire, and the motorway was only ten minutes from home. I could drive to Carlisle or Bristol and back in a day if I wanted and several times I did, with friends who shared the driving.

Now I drive alone. No one here is interested in travelling to distant shows. But here there is peace and a sort of tranquillity. We are remote yet not lonely; there is the village and the phone and we can get out and about. Trials keep me in touch with the world.

Last year most Trials seemed to be in Nottinghamshire. I drove with news of the pit strikes on the radio, to come to roundabouts where there were cones, and we entered down a narrow area and were vetted by the police. I never had any bother; a woman and a dog on their own. A grin and a wave to go on. I passed pits where the pickets stood in rows; and pits where only one or two were visible. I passed an ice-cream van where a policeman, a picket carrying a banner saying 'Coal, not dole' and the ice-cream man sucked cornets and laughed and chatted.

I passed a power station where two policemen leaned against their car and watched pickets playing cricket. I stayed in a hotel right beside a pit entrance; there was no trouble while I was there, although there were reports a week later. I never saw anything but peaceful picketing, and nobody ever interfered with cars passing by, however close.

One of our dog club members was a policeman. We never saw him during the strike - he was on duty almost continuously.

It was a very odd year for everyone.

This place made it seem remote. I look out on to fields, nothing but fields. A few weeks ago they were white with blossom and as I write they are summer green, and it is just after Midsummer Day. A dull day in a dull summer; clouds and rain almost all the time.

The cuckoo that drove us mad a few weeks ago has gone, to our relief, as he started yelling at five and woke Chita who called to be let out, sure it was time to get up. Pheasants sound like gongs. Partridges, crazy birds, nest in the long grass and startle us by rising suddenly and, before I realise what has happened, Chita has eaten their eggs. They never seem to learn.

The kestrel hovers beyond the hedge. The owl hunts by day, and today flew over at ten am. The pheasants have chicks in the field on the other side of the river. The herons fly past regularly to their own hunting grounds, not far from our boundary. Shelduck, with their brilliant orange chests, court on our marsh field. There is a weasel in the flower bed. We rarely see him, but he leaves traces that Chita tracks at night.

When it snowed he came out and the snow blocked his hole, which is in the flower bed. He ran round, demented, while we watched. We were lunching. He tried the back door, looking for shelter; he tried to climb down the drain. He ran in circles and suddenly his paw went into his hole and he vanished. We could imagine his relief. Home at last. He didn't come out again until the snow had gone.

We never know what we will see next. Last year a hen harrier came to eat the mountain ash berries; a handsome bird, big as a peregrine falcon. Last year too there was a plague of jays, as many as our magpies. This year I have seen none. There are grasshopper warblers whirring in the hedges; and tits of all kinds, and chaffinches and bullfinches.

Chita ignores the birds when we are working. A partridge can rise a few feet from her when she is jumping and she does not even look towards the whirring wings. Once, walking with Janus down a lane I came on a dead partridge. Janus sniffed it and I bent over it, wondering if it had been shot. It was shamming.

It flew up into my face. Janus barked and I jumped, and the bird flew over the hedge. I don't know which of the three of us was more startled.

On an autumn day driving past a stubble field, I counted nearly a hundred cock pheasants. The pheasants at Plas Newydd, which are reared for shooting, jaywalk all summer. The young birds stroll across the road and when a car comes they seem paralysed with fright and may freeze. I am forever braking for young pheasants. I have learned never to go fast there, although I am often overtaken and hope I won't see a dead bird lying in the road as I have on several occasions.

Walking Janus near there last year he found a hen pheasant and a clutch of chicks. She flew, the chicks froze, and though I knew they were there, within feet of me, I couldn't see one of them, their camouflage is so perfect. We were in a tiny wood just off the main road.

In autumn too a sign appears near my home.

SLOW - TOADS CROSSING

Hedgehogs run across our garden; they die here too, perhaps from warfarin poisoning, perhaps from some strange hedgehog epidemic. One night I let Janus out, and he vanished. I found him by the gate, poking his paw at a hedgehog. I had to drag him in.

I let Puma out for her turn and she homed in on the scent, right up the field two hundred yards from the house. She sniffed around, but came when I called her. She was blind then and tired as she had the beginnings of liver and kidney cancer and some kind of brain trouble, although I didn't know that at the time.

Chita raced up fast and barked at this odd object and being Chita stabbed her nose on its spines and yelled about that too. She too was dragged in, and I had to take all three out again one by one on the lead for their last emptying, or they would never have done anything. That enticing smell called them and they couldn't bear to leave it alone.

Warfarin is a hazard here as soon after we moved both cats became ill. Casey, who died four years ago, had a sub normal temperature; Chia's was high. They lay, listless, refusing all food. With both cats displaying different symptoms my vet got on to it fast. He said that if he had seen only one he might have missed it, but as it was he was positive. Injections of vitamin K prevented them dying, but it was six weeks before they ate properly again and both looked very sorry animals. The vet suspected that they had been eating mice that had taken warfarin. It would be easy to catch a dying mouse.

107

It is a lovely home for dogs, and more and more I longed to have another to replace Janus. Chita seemed subdued and sometimes depressed without him. At first it had been a novelty being only dog; now there was no other dog to share with. Janus had been too old to play in that last year, but he had happily trotted after her and sometimes remembered the eating game where they rolled together and mouthed one another. Sometimes she would try and entice him to play, offering him her bone, ready to run off with it so that he could chase her, as he had done before old age made him slow and weary. She danced a little, or came to him and nudged him, but he only sighed and rolled on to his other hip, and stretched out in the sun. Maybe she had forgotten those days and remembered only that they had had fun together. She would nose the place where he used to lie, wistfully, and look at me.

I wondered what she was trying to say.

Meanwhile she could have small adventures on our own land. Memories of animals that trotted by; tell-tale tracks in the snow; moles tunnelling; molehills to dig at, though I tried to stop her doing that as she would dig at a molehill when she was tracking.

'Untidy thing. Got to make it flat,' and the earth flew until she was satisfied.

Chita's powers of concentration when she does not want to hear are greater than mine!

Next time I would buy a dog that was nothing like her at all: an easy dog to train, a dog I could do far more with than I have ever been able to do with her, as, when Chita is stressed, she still panics, that old nervous breeding betraying her.

She is almost eight and time is running out.

The days pass; the weeks pass; the months pass, much too fast. It is winter again.

Winter; with its howling gales, blustering across our land, screeching banshee-like round the house, whipping against our faces, so that Chita goes out with her head down.

Winter, when I have to drive to dog club down the dark lanes, between high hedges, and often come home with a drifting mist rising from the fields and making life hazardous. Winter when we put on gloves and scarves and woolly hats and track in desolate fields; when we walk in the deserted park and go down to the Straits and look across the grey sea, and see white-capped waves breaking in the swellies and the whirlies where little boats may be trapped and come to grief.

The Community Centre where we trained was too hot often and dogs were lethargic and going outside to our cars was a penance afterwards. Now we have moved to St Mary's Church House which is much bigger but has no heat. We haven't had a winter there yet, but it should be far better for the dogs who are always more energetic in the cold.

Yet there are advantages to winter, as we see sights that we never see in summer, especially when it snows.

Last March, when it snowed, a red fox sauntered along the river bank. He was a big handsome fellow, with a black-tipped tail. A few minutes before I sat down to write this morning, a heron flapped past the window, looking too heavy to fly. His patch is in the river at the edge of my neighbour's sheepfield, which is noisy just now with sheep and their new lambs, calling to one another. My neighbour often is out at night, in the field the other side of our hedge, supervising his lambing ewes. There are new lambs daily in the fields across the tiny river; no more than a big ditch in the dry days, but often swollen and yellow, rushing over the banks and flooding our lower field, so that instead of grass and reeds there is a steely coloured lake, bleak and forbidding; a constant reminder of winter.

Chapter Twelve

Chita is a showoff. She loves to run around with a large branch in her mouth (no small sticks for Chita!), swanking for all she is worth. So when we were thinking of doing a cover picture for *A Dog in a Million*, I suggested to Seán that we tried to get her to perform with her tree trunk.

He was doubtful, but we went to the Botanic gardens and there we discovered that the problem wasn't to get her to perform, but to stop her performing. Seán wanted her to play with her stick, so play she would, long after we needed the game.

The game, however, took over, and she raced about, showing off for all she was worth. 'Look at me. Aren't I clever?' She did pose problems as she was moving so fast, and often just as Seán was about to take her picture she turned her tail and chased off in the opposite direction.

It was a hilarious session.

Photographic sessions with Chita have always been great fun. She can do any pose; and sparkles with delight for Seán. She became more and more wound up, racing with her tree trunk, charging at us and dodging, but, when we called her to face the camera, she seemed to know exactly what we wanted and immediately posed herself in quite the most effective way.

A couple of years ago I tried to make a video of my book *How To Get a Sensible Dog*. This proved difficult as we were all amateurs and once the video was taped, it was very obvious we were amateurs. Also Chita seemed determined to prove how not to get a sensible dog. We needed a producer and an editor who understood dogs and that seems an impossibility. If ever such people appeared the TV programmes we get about dogs would improve a hundredfold. None is as good as *One Man and His Dog* which is exceptional.

I had a number of incidents on film which would have illustrated what I wanted perfectly, but my editor thought they would give the wrong impression as they showed the dog misbehaving, with me correcting her. All dogs misbehave; it is very little use showing new owners a perfectly trained dog.

It is far better to be bringing up a pup yourself and show them how difficult it is to train the raw material, as your much-older paragon makes them feel inferior. It's so easy when the dog is already trained to put it in a position, such as sit, stand, or down.

It is a very different matter with a fellow that hasn't even had a lead on him by the time he is a year old and is resisting to the top of his bent.

Dogs also know people very much better than people know dogs. A friend of mine married a man who owned two quite old rescued Red Setters. They behaved for him. When the new wife, the intruder into this establishment of one man and two dogs, was cooking supper the dogs made a point of getting in her way, deliberately. The more agitated she became the more they enjoyed it, until in the end she completely lost her calm and yelled at them.

Along came master.

'Lie down at once.'

They did, with an amused eye on her saying 'you can't cope with us, can you?' They have now gone to wherever all dogs go in the end. I hope to fields and rivers and plenty of fun, to be waiting for their owners when their turn comes. My friends have a new rescued animal now, a delightful little German Shepherd bitch. She has only known them as a couple and there is no problem with her at all.

Club at present has a number of rescued dogs, or dogs that have been sold by their first owners for a variety of reasons. Most common are the show dogs. Breeders keep several from every litter, in the hope that this pup or that will make a Champion. Champions aren't thick on the ground, so as they grow disappointment sets in and the pups are sold on.

This can mean problems for new owners as most are kennel-kept, and to change a kennel dog to a house dog is extremely difficult. For one thing few breeders bother to train dogs to be kennel clean, so they aren't used to a routine whereby they have to hang on, and floors in a house suffer. Puma was kennel clean, mostly, although we had a few accidents at first as she was seventeen months old when I took her home, and we weren't used to one another.

It was months before she would come into a house without being terrified of the sights and sounds. She didn't know about vacuum cleaners, or curtains that sometimes were across the window and sometimes were open, and made a funny noise when they moved, as well as a sudden unexpected movement. She knew nothing about taps and running water, or the sound of a cistern flushing.

She knew nothing about radios and TV sets that talked to her or flashed at her; to the end of her life she moved suspiciously past any new box, in case it suddenly spoke, or had pictures.

She had lived her young life in a small cage, with a run, with bars in front of her. She only felt safe in a corner of the dining room with a barricade of chairs round her. I gradually made the space more roomy. The chairs went further and further away from her, creeping an inch or two each day, until at last I could take them away altogether and she behaved like a normal house dog.

She had, however, had one supreme advantage over many kennelled dogs in that she had an excellent breeder who valued her dogs, and they were always treated with kindness. Not all dogs are so lucky.

She had been to shows and she had been socialised in outdoor places. When I visited her, in the intervals between my visits to my dying father (he had stomach cancer), she came out with Janus and me in the car. She walked round Knutsford, which was fun for both of us as she was fascinated by shops.

She would stare with utter incredulity into a shop window full of furniture, her favourite display, and then look at me with amazement in her eyes. She had very large eyes, not characteristic of her breed, but I thought them gorgeous. They were very

112

expressive eyes, so that it was particularly sad when she went blind, as Puma did so enjoy seeing things.

I can never pass a furniture shop these days without remembering the beautiful puppy at my side so absorbed in the mystery of all these strange objects, beyond her understanding, with unimaginable uses. Some of them she met when she did come home. Others neither she nor I had a use for.

None of my other dogs have ever wanted to window gaze. Janus hated shop windows; he seemed more aware of cars reflected in them, flashing past. Chita seems to pretend they aren't really there.

When Janus died Chita was forlorn and I started something with her that I had done with Janus long ago. All my dogs have to come with me on publicity occasions. They must be used to strange places so I always took Janus to Steiner's, the hairdresser at the Midland Hotel in Manchester. Chita now comes to the hairdresser here, where all the staff love her.

It all began by accident. I had only had Janus a few weeks, when I had to go to a bookshow in Liverpool, for Corgi. Richard Robins, their publicity manager, picked me up in his car. Janus could stay in the car, as I couldn't leave him at home.

We were at a college. It was a hot day and the car was hot, although in the shade. But shade moves, so Richard asked the college authorities if we could bring Janus in. They agreed.

Up to then we had had very little interest from the children as another paperback firm was there. They had clown cutouts and balloons and all sorts of gimmicks. They were doing a roaring trade and Richard and I were sitting looking at one another and at a pile of unsold books.

I brought Janus in.

He was delighted to be with us, instead of alone in the car, and being still a puppy, though a big one, he explored the room, and put his nose into the corridor. A small boy saw him and there was a yell.

'There's a puppy.'

In no time at all the children had deserted the clowns and the balloons and were vying to cuddle Janus. He, being the kind of dog that thrives on fussing, sat like an amiable teddy bear, his tail wagging, a grin on his face, in a dog's heaven.

All these people just for him.

Some even bought books.

I was thought to have done it deliberately, but in those days I hadn't realised how animals upstage people.

Chita does it all the time. She did it throughout our video filming, by improvising some absurdity, just as we thought we had a fantastic sequence. One day we decided that as one sequence was long we would put an advertisement in, and see if perhaps the product maker would allow us to use it; maybe they would even pay for its use, as we were very short of funds.

Chita jumped over her hurdle, and came to me when called. The camera had a built-in microphone, so I said: 'If you want a fit dog you want *this* dog food,' and held the tin out for Chita to take as we had rehearsed her trotting to her dinner plate with it.

She looked at it and, very thoughtfully, made a large puddle at my feet before taking the tin and continuing with the sequence.

Needless to say we abandoned that idea!

Old dogs grow very wise: they know what happens and what doesn't happen. Younger dogs tend to take things in their stride as their minds are like sponges and there is so much to learn about the world.

When I took the three dogs to the Children's Book Fair at Liverpool Cathedral when Chita was only sixteen weeks old, the two older dogs could not take the Dr Who monsters, the Daleks, or the eight-foot-high kangaroo. Puma was terrified of them. These strange objects were entirely new to her, and they threatened her. She crawled under a table and lay there, her eyes wild.

Worst of all was Snoopy, parading round the floor, doing ballet steps. I put Puma in the car. It was sanctuary to her, a mobile kennel, away from all the noise, the racing children, the strange monsters.

Janus found an echo and wouldn't stop barking. The monsters worried him too, but not to excess. The echo fascinated him.

114

'Woof.' And the walls woofed back. Another dog? Or did he know it was his own voice replying? Whatever it was he wouldn't stop. He sat there, interrogating the echo, until he too had to go in the car.

Chita meanwhile was so young that everything was new to her.

She met mysteries daily.

Bicycles; cars at night that roared towards her with their great eyes glowing; strange things that happened in the garden. One day Philip, who helps us with our unruly plot, decided that the rhododendrons needed protecting against the weather. He made a tent of wood and polythene. I didn't see this happen, and let Chita out that night as usual.

She found an 'intruder' in the garden and roared at it. I raced out with the torch to find her barking madly at the rhododendron shelter. It was some days before she accepted that as part of her familiar landscape. She was much older then.

As a pup she was merely curious. What were these things? Smell them. Smell like people, so wag tail and fuss them. She stood up against a green Dr Who monster, looking extremely funny as she was so tiny and it was both big and extremely weird.

So she stayed and was fussed and petted, which was extremely good for her as when she came to me she appeared to loathe people. At that age she could take a great deal in the way of new and unfamiliar objects; they were just part of the world that she hadn't yet met and anything might happen.

As she grew older she too found that new experiences caused her more worry. She knew her world and the objects she met frequently. She has no phobias, unlike Janus, who when I got him at five months old, was petrified beyond all reason if he met a milk float, or, even odder, a World Wildlife panda collecting box. The panda is large with a baby in its arms and the big box fixed to it, and there was one outside a local shop. Nothing I could do ever got him past it. We had to cross the road. As we went that way daily, I had to remember. He sat and shook and refused to move, and as he weighed around eighty pounds there was little I could do about that.

The difference in the way pups and adult dogs behave showed up last year.

I was sitting in our morning room having a leisurely breakfast, Chita at my side. Kenneth was taking the bag of rubbish up the lane to put out for the binmen.

Quite suddenly Chita stood, rushed to me and thrust her head into my lap, trembling. Her eyes were agonised and something was frightening her very badly. A few moments later, I knew what it was, but not what was causing it. The whole house shook; there was a tremendous noise, as if a jetplane had just crashed into our back garden, and then a long thunder rumble, but the thunder came from all around us, underneath as well as in the air.

Windows and doors and glassware rattled.

I thought World War Three had started. Somewhere an atomic bomb had gone off; or Wylva Power Station, which is nuclear, had blown up. I was probably as scared as Chita, I'd never experienced anything like it either.

Kenneth came in and we speculated as to what on earth had caused the effect. After about two minutes everything was still again. It was not until later that day, hearing the one o'clock news, that we realised there had been an earthquake and we were only a few miles from its epicentre. It had been quite severe.

We had several more and each time Chita warned me that they were about to happen and we went outside. One, a few weeks later, started just after we had gone to bed, and from downstairs came an unhappy howling. It is the only time she has been allowed to sleep with us. She lay on the rug by my bed, and when the little quakes came, a small black nose thrust at me and she sat, asking to be reassured. She knew that the earth didn't normally behave like that.

When the quakes stopped some weeks later as the earth settled, she returned to her own bed downstairs without any problem.

The butcher in the next village was eating his breakfast when the quake began and his large Labrador landed in his lap. One little Sheltie had just gone outside to spend a penny when the quake began. She fled to a corner of the garden and crouched there, and for some days was very reluctant to go outside again at all. Noises happened when you spent pennies these days!

Yet pups under six months old weren't in the least bothered. This was just something else that happened in the strange world in which they found themselves.

We take so much for granted. Dogs can only accept what they know, and even an old dog may need reassuring. I was once walking in a wood with Janus when we caught up with a man carrying a small child. The dog sat and refused to go on.

I couldn't imagine what was wrong with him and then I saw the man's shadow. A man with two heads.

I called out to him.

'I'm sorry. Would you mind turning round so that my dog can see your little boy? He can't make out what is wrong with you as he's never seen anyone carry a child before.'

The man turned round and grinned at me. Janus looked up at me with an expression that said: 'Made a fool of myself then, didn't I?' and we passed the man, thanking him, and went on.

I once rode a very wise old horse who baulked at nothing. Or so they said.

One day Beau and I were ambling along the lane when I saw a man in a hole in the road. So did Beau, but what he saw was a man without legs, and he began to dance. It was very difficult to ride him, so I called out to the man:

'My horse is frightened of you, would you mind coming out of the hole very slowly and standing still?'

Luckily he was a countryman and did as I asked. Beau watched him, and then turned his head and looked at me. 'How did he do that?' We walked on, and the horse stopped for a fuss and a pat, and I am sure he looked sheepish, having realised he had made a mistake and thought there was only half a man in the road.

I often feel people don't think themselves into the animal's

117

skin. We can never explain to a dog, it's OK, we'll be coming back in an hour. Until the dog has learned that you do leave him alone and *do* come back again, he feels abandoned. Puppies have to be taught that they must be alone sometimes; but when starting with a new pup it's best to let them be alone for only a few minutes at a time, and keep returning; then the time can be extended.

Otherwise you get a dog that can't be left at all, and that gives the family major problems.

Few people realise what an immense amount of time has to be spent in training a dog. A dog that lives in the house is relatively easier, as that has to accept household noises and comings and goings, and is under your eye all the time so that you can take steps to correct it. For instance when the doorbell rings.

What should be done is what few of us ever think of doing or find time for. The training situation has to be set up, with co-operative and knowledgeable people. They aren't easy to find.

The dog is sat, on the lead, and the doorbell rung. The dog is kept sitting and the check chain tightened and immediately loosened again with the sharp word 'NO' as he barks. This has to be repeated and repeated until in the end you have won the battle and the dog knows that when people come to the door of the house, he sits to greet them, and behaves himself.

It is much easier said than done.

Also if you backslide, then the dog does too. It has to be repeated daily as does all training, or the dog takes over and does as it likes and that can be dangerous at times.

Chita always leaped at Liz, who comes for two hours daily to do chores that would prevent me writing if I had to do them myself. I was never quick enough to stop her. Then it dawned on me that as soon as the doorbell rang Chita had to go on the lead, come to the door, be quiet, sit while I opened it and greet Liz sanely.

It took some weeks; both of us having to work on the dog. It needs cooperation, just as when a police dog is being trained for manwork the partner who acts the part of the criminal trains the dog, not only the man handling the dog.

Many dog training situations need a cooperative partner who understands dogs, which is why so many of us fail to achieve a degree of control that would come far more easily if we had skilled friends.

Sometimes family members sabotage all efforts, which is heartbreaking. The dog is controlled by one person, who spends hours training and does his or her best to ensure the animal becomes a useful family companion. The rest of the family do their best to undo all the hard work put in and so ruin the dog. They play the wrong games with it, tease it, teach it to tug and tear, and then blame the dog's owner for things they themselves have caused.

One club member came to me very worried. His young son had been playing ball with his large male German Shepherd dog. The dog had become hooked on the ball and the boy teased him with it by holding it up in the air above his head and pretending to throw it, but not doing so.

The dog's owner knew nothing of this as it happened while he was at work. He took the dog for a walk one day, and a child got out of a car with a ball, went to throw it and the dog grabbed his arm, wanting the ball. The dog didn't bite, just held the arm, but it terrified the child and his parents and it terrified the dog's owner.

The game had to stop and fast, or that dog might well have caused a disaster, not intentionally, but because some child ran from the animal hanging on to the ball and the dog tried to get it.

If the child resisted, or fell . . .

It is very easy to say there are no bad dogs, only bad owners. Nobody can teach a skill they haven't been taught. You might just as well say I am ignorant because I don't speak Greek, Japanese and Chinese. Yes, I am, but nobody has taught it to me so how can I know it?

Life is too short for any of us to become experts in everything. I will never win Cruft's Obedience. I will probably never qualify Chita in Trials. I doubt if any Cruft's winner will ever write the kind of books I write. Nobody shines at everything.

This doesn't make any of us the lesser person. How many of those reading this book would make a good saddler or a good blacksmith? Or become a chef at the Ritz?

A good shepherd is unlikely to train his dog for criminal work; few police dogs could round up sheep; yet those writing books on dog training make glib statements indicating that anybody ought to be able to train a dog without being instructed, except in a few brief lessons over a period of perhaps ten weeks. Which is utterly crazy.

Very few people seem to know enough about the mentality of a dog to understand how to train it. It is a very simple animal, yet it can reason up to a point.

It can't know it mustn't chase sheep if it has never been stopped. Though I don't allow my dogs to chase, they will revert and I don't trust any dog, however well trained, to resist temptation one hundred times out of one hundred.

If a dog does chase and I am there, it is my fault; I shouldn't have let it off lead.

If it chases and I am not there then I am abdicating from my responsibility which is to keep my dog under control at all times, and on my premises. It is an offence to let a dog wander, and even if it isn't by law, it ought to be. I see too many sheep mauled by dogs; they go for the throat and the stomach and, having torn out their guts, leave them alive. Nobody would believe their charming little dog would do such a thing, but dogs don't know about right or wrong. We have to be responsible and if we aren't, then there is trouble and it is our fault.

Chita lives with the cat; she knows very well she is not allowed to chase it, but if the cat runs she *will* chase and I can't stop her till I have caught up with her. She chases other cats if they come on to our field. I can't teach her to leave every single individual cat alone. If I see a cat in time I can shout 'NO' and drop her; and nine times out of ten she drops. The tenth, she doesn't.

She's a dog, not a robot. No dog is perfect and nor is any human. I ought not to eat chocolate; I sometimes do, and I am a reasoning creature aware that it causes me problems as I am mildly allergic to it and can feel sick after eating it.

I always hope that this time it won't have that effect, just as Chita always hopes that this time she'll get away with chasing the cat and I won't stop her.

So the training has to begin again.

Training can never stop. Dogs don't learn for life. They do learn by experience what is wise to do and what is not. If they find they can steal your dinner and not be stopped while in the act, they'll try again. They'll behave guiltily when they realise you are angry; they won't know *why* you are angry.

Suppose someone came racing into the room with a knife and threatened you for no reason at all other than that they happened to be insane? You wouldn't sit there calmly aware you had done no wrong so wouldn't be hurt. You'd be terrified even though it was crazy. The dog recognises your fury from your behaviour; you are tense and your voice is loud. He reacts to that. The stolen food or the chewed-up shoe has long been forgotten. What's wrong *now?* No idea!

It isn't always easy to live with a dog happily; those who do have learned a skill that newcomers take years to acquire. Some never know that there is a skill to acquire.

A dog will copy the worst dog around; that gets away with murder and so, he thinks, can he. Just as children will copy bad behaviour; they see people on strike or throwing petrol bombs, so they do too. Children need heroes to copy; if they don't have them they copy what they see.

Few people ever see a really well trained dog, so they don't know that their dogs are at fault, racing out and barking at people, racing up to other dogs and trying to fight them.

They say 'dogs do that'. They only do it because nobody trains them.

Chapter Thirteen

One of the highlights in our dog club each year is the sponsored downstay for our Guide Dogs for the Blind fund. There is very little to pull a club together when people only meet once a week to train their dogs, so it has always seemed to me very worthwhile to have a common aim which interests everybody.

We have several blind people in our area, all using guide dogs, so that it is easy to find one of them to come to club and talk. Our first guide dog was achieved in 1982.

Her name is Freya, in memory of a club dog that died tragically at just over a year old. We were sent her photograph. She is a pretty German Shepherd bitch, rather like Chita to look at, sitting in a field against a background of winter trees, wearing her harness.

Like Chita, she is alert, eager, and her beautiful eyes are focussed sideways from the camera, presumably on her owner.

Arthur Rowlands, who has recently retired from the Caernarfon police force, came to accept the first cheque. He was blinded by a man with a shotgun some years ago and his guide dog, also a German Shepherd, brought him to us. He gave us an insight into the freedom that can be achieved with a dog, as opposed to having to rely on a human guide, who may not always be free. The dog is with you twenty-four hours a day and always willing to come and guide his master.

It is far from easy to collect the necessary £1000 and our reward is that photograph and the caption beneath it, as well as the immense satisfaction of having made such an effort. The caption reads:

Presented to
BANGOR CITY DOG TRAINING CLUB
in gratitude by the
Guide Dogs for the Blind Association

We collected the money for that particular dog in a variety of ways.

We held a weekly raffle for one of my books. This sounds like self-advertising, but I can get my books at trade price, which means that we had only a small outlay. A book selling at £1.50 costs me £1.00 and we usually raised £4 or £5 for it.

Members held coffee mornings, and one sold Christmas cards from one of the organisations that give 25 per cent of the profits to charity.

The sponsored downstay always raised most money. The dogs have to lie still without moving for ten minutes. The downstay isn't the easiest of exercises to teach but when members realised that their dogs could earn money for charity by teaching it, they worked hard, and no dog has ever failed to stay the full time.

Most members take part. Those that work for big organisations like the Post Office are lucky and Bangor Post Office in particular has contributed a considerable sum to our guide dogs through various past members whose husbands worked there.

Last year I sent Chita's sponsor forms to two of my publishers and my agent and Chita was able to collect nearly £200. I haven't had the nerve to repeat this exercise; they might get tired of me! Chita has never broken her sponsored downstay or stays in club or practice. She feels secure there and of course my people train my way and don't bawl and bellow at their dogs.

We usually asked our president to monitor the stays and see that we did not cheat. Mrs Christie, a very charming lady who had been Mayor of Bangor several times, was president. She came, looking lovely, and watched for us and signed all the forms.

Very sadly she died last year and as her particular fund had been for the restoration of Bangor pier to its former glory, that year we gave a percentage of our sponsor money to the pier fund in her memory. We have a very handsome certificate acknowledging our gift which is in the club photograph album. I keep records of press cuttings about the club and photographs of club dogs.

Just before the 1984 guide dog sponsored down, the chaplain from RAF Valley, Bob Bailey, joined the club with his Labrador Bess. Bess, who is black and as beautiful as all Labs, chose to come straight into season, so he rang to say he would not be in for the next three weeks.

I asked if he would monitor the stays for us and he came over from Valley to do so. He was fascinated to discover how steady the dogs were and how short a time some of them had been training. We were now well on the way to collecting our second £1000.

Valley is well over twenty miles from Bangor, and while he was chatting with us, Bob discovered that several members of Bangor dog club came from Holyhead, or places near to it. He asked if I would consider opening another class at Valley, at the RAF Community Centre. Nothing to pay for the venue, and the money, apart from £2 for my petrol, could go to the guide dog fund and make that second guide dog a reality much sooner. I would have no responsibility other than to teach, and to bank the guide dog money. He would do everything else.

I thought about it. Valley would be on Monday and only for one hour. Bangor was overfull and I had no experienced help at all. It is very hard to find people qualified to teach and with enough dog background to allow them responsibility. They need to be gentle with people as well as dogs, and many good dog handlers get impatient with inexperienced owners.

Most of us in dogs are amateurs; there are very few real professionals.

Most specialise in one or two fields only. You can have all-rounders in related fields; the basics of guide dog, police dog and pet dog training are the same. Nobody would go to a man who trains sheepdogs to learn how to train a police dog, or vice versa. Very few have dual skills.

Anyone can decide to be a professional and set up a plate without any experience at all. Some of them ought to be drummed out of the business. I could, by taking money for lessons and club, become an instant professional. I have more experience in dogs than some 'professionals' and probably wouldn't be as much of a fraud as some of them. But I don't want to earn my living that way; I prefer to keep dogs for fun.

I have now learned not to take people at their own valuation, but to ask around. When did that one start in business? What was he or she doing before? One instant expert had owned a small breed of dog for two years and set up as an 'experienced' breeder. Another breeder, quoted often to me as having more knowledge than I, beat her bitch for licking up the pups excrement and for vomiting back her food to wean them. She was totally unaware that this is natural dog behaviour. Wild dogs do it to keep the nest clean and when she whelps the bitch reverts to the wild instincts.

Many a person has been bitten by a bitch with pups because the 'breeder' was so inexperienced that she or he had no idea that bitches do protect their babies with their teeth, and mean business. I never count a bite in that situation as a sign of vice; it's a sign of a very good mother! We can't expect an animal to adopt human criteria.

I called in at one kennels and was asked if I would like to see the pups. Who can resist that?

I was sure they were all experienced, but someone took the bitch off the pups and let her out into the yard where I was waiting. She went chump, chump, chump down my leg; luckily I was wearing thick trousers and rain gear over them so she did no more than bruise, but she meant business.

When I visited Eric Roberts a few weeks back and was allowed to see Dusty's pups, I was not able to go in until Dusty had been taken, on her leash, for a walk well away from the kennels. I was not even allowed out of the house till she had gone and was well away from the area. She never had bitten anyone in defence of her pups, but Eric takes no chances. Bitches with babies may well be unable to prevent that strong protective instinct taking over. Dusty also knows the pups go away from her after a few weeks, and may well resent people who come to visit in case they go away too soon.

Puma was whelped by Judy Pilling, who bred her; and I wasn't allowed to see Puma with her pups; she was taken away

125

when I visited them. And she was my own bitch. You can tell the real dyed-in-the-wool professional with experience when you know about dogs.

Dusty's recent litter of six pups is lovely and one of my neighbours is having one of them so I will see it grow up. She is due to collect any day now and is so excited about her first German Shepherd that she rings me to talk about the expected newcomer. Eric will have news of that one from me, and the little one is going to a good home. Maybe she too will join the club and one day take part in our sponsored downstay.

I thought over Bob Bailey's suggestion. Bangor club night was Tuesday, so I would be free from Wednesday to Sunday. It would save several of my members coming so far, and I would get my petrol money back so wouldn't be out-of-pocket. I decided to try for a few weeks. In the end I stayed there for nearly thirteen months.

Then, as our Bangor club venue had risen in price and was £12 a night, we moved to our present venue which is only £5 a night. Unfortunately we had to change to Thursday, which meant my week was now broken up into two halves and I was never free to go away for more than a couple of days. This made going to Trials difficult. Several times I was given a Friday track, and I just couldn't get there.

Someone else had come to join Valley and help with the training, so I gave up to concentrate on the Bangor club again, and extend its activities, as we are now collecting for our third guide dog. We took four years to get Freya, two years to get the second and now we want £1000 in one year.

Valley did contribute over £300 towards the second, as I often brought home £12 or more a night, but that split week was tiresome and there weren't really enough people per night for three of us.

I was sorry to leave as I had become attached to my small group of 'regulars', but there were a great many new people who I barely know, as they had joined just before I decided to resign.

For the first few weeks there were only a few handlers: Bob

126

Bailey, the chaplain, with Bess; Pip who was in charge of the helicopters for search and rescue, with his yellow Labrador, Prince, a lively fellow with bags of character; another Bob with his German Shepherd, Ben. Ben was a handful, but Bob proved an apt pupil and when I left I was able to send him a progress prize, as he worked on that dog and Ben was becoming far easier. I hope he has stayed that way. I have a very soft spot for Ben, and for Bob, who experienced many of the problems I had with Chita, so I could sympathise fully with him.

That little group proved very rewarding. There was Dorothy with her mischievous little West Highland Terrier, Dougal. He was adorable, but so naughty. Like many Terriers he rebelled by growling if he didn't want to work, and Dorothy had to learn to overcome that and not allow it to happen.

Trish, with her yellow Labrador, Lucy, insisted on telling me she couldn't work her dog; they had no chance at all in the certificate test; and then she came up with over 90 per cent twice! Another 90 per cent and she would have a diploma. I shouldn't have told her that as Trish wanted it so badly and was so tense it reacted on Lucy and they went down. It took another twelve weeks for Trish to come back into working without worry again and sail through to earn her diploma.

While I was at Valley I wrote out a questionnaire for both clubs to help me know more about each one and where the dogs lived, as it is one thing to live on a terraced street in a town and another in an isolated cottage in the country. Another club member, Gabriella, lives in an old farmhouse right down on the beach. She is cut off at high tide, or was until this year when a road was put through the fields. She came to club with wellingtons in the car so that she and Tess could wade home, leaving the car on the road until the tide went down. It always seemed to me a singularly uncomfortable way to live.

Yet she came in the worst of weather when those off-sea winds must have made her walk in the winter dark along the beach extremely unpleasant.

One of the questions I asked was: 'How much time each day do you spend training?'

127

Trish wrote: 'I am embarrassed to find I don't spend any time training Lucy, yet I seem to train her all day, as each new situation we come to seems to need a little bit of training, although not done the way we do it in club.'

She was the only member out of about sixty who did what I was trying to teach! Others taught heelwork in class and walked out with dogs still pulling the owners off their feet, and choking themselves.

It is very difficult to get over that the work done is to apply in real life, and not just on Thursday night in class, for a certificate at the end of it. We are now adding roadwork to our proficiency certificate to see if owners do apply what they have learned elsewhere.

Valley continued to thrive. Julie changed from Bangor to Valley with her delightful German Shepherd bitch, Kizzie. Kizzie is small and dainty and charming, working extremely well. Wenda came with her Collie cross, Megan, another charmer who walked off with many prizes while I was there. Megan is pretty and tiny and, like all Collies, delights in working, even if it is only pretend work at club and elsewhere.

I enjoyed Valley very much indeed; they worked hard, were keen and great fun. They also gave me an insight into another way of life, although it's a way of life I personally would detest.

My first glimpse of it was through Julie Dane, who in fact had been a private pupil before I started the RAF Valley group and had spoken to the chaplain to suggest a dog club there, as the station, which is immense, seethes with dogs. Julie had been my Weightwatchers lecturer and had enabled me to lose an unwanted stone. She couldn't come to dog club as it was the same night as her classes.

She had two Shelties, Princess and Mischief, who were, she said, both awkward. She came for about seven weeks with them and we made immense progress. It was great fun, as by then I knew Julie well and we always ended our sessions with coffee. Then she came with sad news for me.

Her husband, who is a Squadron Leader in the RAF, had

been posted to Cyprus for five years. So off they went, with the dogs.

Then Keith joined with a Labrador, lasted five weeks and was posted to an aircraft carrier. Kevin was posted to Germany after only two weeks. Bob Bailey vanished in January to the Falklands.

They are forever on the move.

They live in furnished houses; pack up and leave, taking it for granted that they are here today and gone tomorrow, never putting down roots, perhaps never making real friends, never able to settle anywhere.

I had more than a glimpse of that when the station changed its Commandant and Derek and Judy arrived at club with their gorgeous Druidswood German Shepherd puppy Zak. Zak started as a tiny object, small and adorable. He sat, staring, very much in awe of all those enormous dogs, with ears that didn't always remember to stand erect so that he had a cock-eyed baby look about him.

Within a surprisingly few weeks he was an enormous gangly fellow, full of life and fun, and is now a maturing handsome dog, very rewarding indeed.

Judy and Derek have lived all over the world: in Tel Aviv; in the Arizona desert, when Derek was on loan to the United States Air Force; in remote places and huge cities; always in furnished accommodation; sometimes in stately embassy houses. At Valley they have a house bigger than the rest but it is very much an RAF barracks home.

It is on the station which is so vast that it is like a town, with its own shops and a great many clubs, for golf, for cricket, for football, for rugby; a sergeants' mess; a community centre; an officers' mess. You name it, it's there, as well as the little church and a theatre. We went in through a road labelled 'M.O.D. Keep Out'. Nobody ever challenged me unless I had to go on to the airfield, when you do have to see the guards and have passes.

They are of course guarded, especially nowadays. All through the winter, after the bombing of the Brighton Hotel where the Prime Minister and her entourage were staying, the camp was

129

on amber alert. There were always guards on all the entrances and it was a case of pass and be recognised. With Chita in the back of my car I was soon waved on.

We had to negotiate a maze of barbed-wire barricades. As it was winter and dark this wasn't too easy. I shall never forget those winter drives along the coast with the wind howling and snow in the air, and the sea hurling itself against the beaches; the dark moors, where mists rose and drifted past the car; the lonely narrow road, where I rarely saw another vehicle.

Part of it was moorland where sheep and cattle have commonland grazing and I had to watch for their bodies blundering across the road.

The patchwork lights of the isolated farms were all that convinced me Chita and I weren't the only creatures alive on those desolate roads.

The summer roads are another thing with daylight and gorse blazing and bright skies and blue seas with small crested waves; with the beaches inviting, and the moorlands flower-covered, and people on holiday.

I was also made very aware of the role of 22 Squadron who are concerned with search and rescue. Pip was in charge of heli-copter maintenance and as the helicopter hangar was near where we worked, we knew the vehicles had always to be in perfect repair, ready to go out the second there was a call. They have recently completed their three thousandth rescue.

They are in touch round the clock with the police and the civilian mountain rescue teams, who use dogs to find victims. Police dogs may be brought in to search too. They must be very highly trained, safe with animals, and as easily able to find a lost climber or child as arrest a villain.

The helicopters fly over our home to reach the mountains, and when they have flown past, I search the papers next day.

One week this year they went out three days running, and each time took a dead man off the mountain. Mountain victims are usually those who have no respect for the hills. They are often ill-prepared, wearing jeans and tee-shirts and plimsolls, unaware that high up it can be winter cold, even in summer, with ice and snow and gale-force winds that kill fast, especially if you fall and are injured.

When I was in college long ago the student who sat next to me in class went out one icy winter night to climb by moonlight. He was ill-prepared, and fell. He had told no one where he was going. He broke his ankle. This was long before dogs were used on the hills. They found him three days later, suffering from exposure. Had they found him at once he'd have lived, but he died. He died on Tryfan and I was told that Tryfan claims a life a year.

These days all the hills seem to claim a good many lives each year. Our hospital specialises in mountain injuries.

Before the Caernarfon and Anglesey hospital was closed and moved to the new site of Ysbyty Gwynedd (which means Gwynedd Hospital), the helicopters used to land on the sports field where Hilary who came to club with her German Shepherd, Lordy, lived. It was near the hospital.

The ambulance came and Hilary gave the crew tea while they waited for the member who had gone with the victim and had to give statements to the police. Her small son, then only five, loved his visitors, although he never knew why they were there. They made a fuss of the small boy. He was very indignant when the new hospital opened, and had a launching pad for the helicopters so that mountain and other victims can go straight there. He lost his tea with the men he so enjoyed meeting and his view of the helicopter itself.

The helicopters may need repairs and then work goes on all night. None of them can be out-of-action.

The men need flying time; they need to practise and one day Derek came in having spent part of the morning in a wet suit in Holyhead harbour, while the crew practised winching him out of the water.

In winter as I turned over in bed at two in the morning, hearing the helicopter engine, while the wind howled and ice formed on the grass, I knew Pip's colleagues were going out again, to contend with wind and weather, as accidents rarely happen in good conditions.

The civilian team would be standing by, the dogs wearing their search harnesses and the heavier jacket with its shackles that enables the dog to be winched in and out of the helicopter.

It must be spooky to lie injured on the mountain and see the green unearthly light on the dog's harness approach, hear a snuffle, and then see the light vanish as the dog, having identified a victim, races to alert his master and bring the medical team. All mountain rescue dog handlers must be grade A climbers and first-class first aid men, and stretcher bearers.

The helicopter crews are so familiar with death. So are the mountain rescue men, who talk of deaths at the pass known as Nameless which sounds to me like the end of the world, creepy and horrible; of deaths on the hills.

Once I was allowed in the control room and looked at the enormous detailed wall map that shows where to go; at the paraphernalia of a service that so many people forget until they are in trouble, floating out to sea in a rubber dinghy; in a sinking yacht; on a ship that has struck rocks; windsurfing, risking their lives, unaware that their folly may cost an innocent man his life.

The helicopter crews and the mountain rescue men don't always come home. In our safe lives we forget the risk-takers; the policemen, the firemen, the helicopter crews, the lifeboat men.

What always seems extraordinary to me is that the lifeboat crews and the mountain rescue crews rely on charity; all their funds come from you and me. Yes, we may need them, if we aren't careful, but if we contribute to them, as we should, we pay for the foolhardy who take major risks and involve others in an expedition that may well end in death.

I miss Valley. It taught me a lot while I was there, and little of it was about dogs.

I taught them too and treasure the letters they wrote when I resigned. I particularly treasure Bob's as he realised that between us we had changed his German Shepherd from a nervous dog lunging at others to a much more secure animal, a joy to live with. Training has done that to Chita too.

Teaching is two way, and the teacher learns as much as the pupils; their dogs taught me too.

I remember them daily as the helicopters come over and I now know the work that goes into keeping those machines airborne, and the preparation that goes into every rescue, as nothing can be left to chance.

I remember the day I went in to teach, at six o'clock, having gone out at two to shop locally, which took ages due to summer visitors and their cars, and raced to dog club. When I arrived Derek said casually that he had just read one of my books. When did he do that? 'This afternoon. I was co-pilot on a flight to Italy and it was a very dull journey.'

He had been to Italy and back while I had driven about twenty-five miles!

It was a very educational few months and it had provided almost a third of the money for guide dog number 2.

We are now on the way to guide dog number 3 and only presented the last cheque three weeks ago, so we are trying to collect for this one in record time; and then for number 4.

I now know another blind man and recently when he came to talk to us I acted as his 'dog', as he lost one recently through old age and doesn't get his new dog for a few weeks yet. He can't wait. I was steering him, with his hands on my shoulders, through a crowded pub. It is remarkably difficult as you have to give information all the time. Straight ahead; be careful, there is a sideboard here with a sharp corner; turn right, avoid the step which goes up; there is a narrow doorway, and now we turn to the left; there is a chair behind you.

The dog does it all with only his harness to guide his owner. He does it so easily; so much more easily than we, who ought to be far more skilled.

There's more to dogs than people think!

Chapter Fourteen

Whoever named Trials Trials should have named them Tribulations. Though our saga of failure may seem unusual, it isn't, as the dogs are being trained up to police dog standard, and in an entry of 40 or more handlers, only about eight will qualify; some days only one or two get the required 80 per cent.

Chita has done all the exercises and gained full marks – but never all at once. Last month I took her to yet another Trial. Our first in 1985.

It was early March and back on my old patch, the tracks being laid near the kennels where Puma was born and where I spent so many years visiting and walking the dogs.

I went over on the Thursday, to stay at the Ellesmere. I was greeted by both Angelas and by Kami, the lovely little German Shepherd bitch that Eric Roberts found for them. Kami was well and truly in season. Luckily Chita is female too.

Eric had recently got engaged, and was to be married at Easter. He and Liz, his fiancée, who I had not yet met, were to come and have a meal with me. The two Angelas knew nothing of the engagement and when I told them, brought out a bottle of champagne which we were to share, to toast them both and wish them happiness.

During the evening, Eric said suddenly: 'Joyce, I've got just the dog for you. He's a lovely fellow; easy to manage and extrovert, and very teachable. His name's Josse.'

I laughed and said: 'Get thee behind me,' but the words stuck. I had no intention whatever of having another dog while Chita was alive, but Chita was nearly eight and would soon have to retire from Trials; even she would age and one day be gone. And I had made up my mind long ago that my next dog would be named Josse after the book I was writing at the time.

'No,' I said.

'He's yours if you want him.'

I went to bed and thought of having another dog; I hadn't time. Had I? It's not much fun sitting every day in front of a word processor for hours on end, and if I cut back the number of articles I did and only wrote one or at most two books a year . . . and did less outside talking and rushing round the country . . . then I did have time.

Time for a new dog; time to learn about him; time to teach him; time to make him friendly with Chita; time to spend out-of-doors, instead of indoors; as Chita even now isn't quite so ready for endless walking and endless training.

I was very tempted indeed. Should I, shouldn't I? Was it daft? How would Chita react? I knew how Kenneth would react, with a loud and vehement no. I lay awake for a long time, but had come to no real conclusion by morning. I still said no.

By the end of the Trials I had convinced myself that it would be silly to have another dog.

Besides, this was no pup but an adult dog, and I knew nothing of his past. Eric knew very little. His first owner had died six months before and he'd had a variety of owners since. The dog had no home now. He was for sale to the first who wanted him. A homeless dog. A nice dog.

But . . . .

Would he train for Trials at all? Eric said Josse wanted to learn, but he knew nothing of his breeding. I might be starting on the same old round all over again, trying to qualify with a dog that had nothing in him that would make him even want to work for me.

Chita has not the right breeding; she has bits of the right breeding, but that isn't what makes a working dog.

I thought of competition; and I thought of a nice dog that would make an easy companion, and blow qualifying. Does it matter so much? It makes no difference to what I know, to what I do, to how I live, except that I enjoy getting away for weekends; and I enjoy training the dog.

Another dog would complicate my life. I would enjoy

training him, yes. I would enjoy him, yes. Chita was, as Chita has always been, a major stumbling block. She had been only dog for a year; she had thrived on it. She had calmed on it. Another dog would upset her beyond measure.

I couldn't have another dog.

Eric had said take your time; think it over. Come and see the dog if you think you are interested. He wasn't pressuring me. I was to see him again on Sunday as he was judging the WD stake at the same Trials and had set out an unusual test.

'Come over and see the track,' he said. The tracking ground was on my way to Lymm, where I was to pick up my daughter and our new grandson and take them home for a few days. I had no need to make up my mind there and now.

Next morning, the Friday, it had snowed; not a very good augury for Trials. We were to track on the Saturday and today I was to visit a friend.

I hoped that this time we might make Chita's qualification. It was probably pie in the sky, but we all go in full of hope. We had worked very hard all winter, but if it continued to snow heavily it was very likely the Trials might be cancelled. A track in snow would be a piece of cake; I could see where it went and surely get her round that!

Snow was driving down in great flakes so I decided to wait till I saw what the weather was going to do before driving to visit Joy. I walked Chita in the snow, which wasn't much fun for either of us as it was bitterly cold, very slippery and the large flakes clung to our faces, so that we both needed to shake them off. I thought, as I walked, about the Trials requirements; how far had my winter training gone?

The walk in the snow proved useful, as I had time to think about Chita's stays. She had had such a major fright on that occasion that so terrified her that she had wet herself. To persist might be cruel. If she would stay then well and good, but if she got up and followed me, there was nothing I could do at a Trial as I can't take her back and put her back and insist she stays when in competition.

I can't possibly punish her for coming to me, as next time she

136

might run off, afraid to stay and afraid of me as well. That would make matters even worse. I could go on trying and hope.

The snow had eased by lunchtime. Dark Angela made me a lovely omelette and then we set off to see Joy. I have stayed with her with all three dogs, a number of times. Chita knew her well, knew the house well, and knew Joy's Shelties well. As we turned into the road where Joy lives, Chita sat up, and looked about her. She began to squeal.

'I know where we are.'

She was out of the car and into the house as soon as Joy opened the door. A brief greeting for Joy and then a race round, sniffing. Where's Glenn? Where's Pepper? Nowhere in the house. Must be in the garden. She asked for the back door to be opened and raced outside. The garden is tiny. Glenn and Pepper had died before Janus, and there was no trace of them anywhere. The house has been recarpeted since they went.

Chita came to lie beside us, head on paws, eyes sad.

No dogs. Where had they gone?

She remained depressed all the time we were there, a small quiet dog, doing as she was told, with all the eagerness gone from her.

Joy and I caught up on news of family, friends and acquaintances, and then it was time to go back to the Ellesmere.

Eric, Liz and I spent the evening talking dog and once more I heard about Josse. And was tempted.

Chita wouldn't like another dog. Kenneth would be violently against another dog. It would complicate my life all over again.

I said no, reluctantly. Very reluctantly.

It was no use. It was impossible.

Next morning I woke up to deep snow again. Were the Trials on or off? Macclesfield is high so maybe it wouldn't be snowing at Mobberley. 'Going?' asked blonde Angela as she served my breakfast. I was going.

Although the paths and gardens were deep in snow, the roads were clear. I left Macclesfield behind me and turned on to the road to Knutsford. Soon there were only traces of snow, but there was snow on the wind. It was mid March and it was cold.

I was back in familiar country. Here I had walked Puma's mother Witch, before the pups were born. I had walked Porky and Panther and Puma and Janus together down that lane. Here was the road that had been resurfaced the day Puma got burned paws from something spilled on the surface.

It was haunted country.

I turned down the lane that led to the Railway Inn which was the base for the day. I met Val whose dog is like Chita, a madcap type, unpredictable, difficult, always getting full marks for most exercises and then blowing one that he has never failed before. Just like Chita.

She had a new young dog and I was envious.

It was still snowing slightly. I was to track at eleven and it was nine-thirty. I looked at the jumps. They were white. White against white snow. There was still some green grass. Chita's agility is her best exercise. Better do the control work now and get it over before it really snows.

Heelwork; she can do that. I set off confidently. So did Chita, about twice as fast as I was going. I brought her back to heel. She behaved as if she had never been taught. We then had to make a figure of eight pattern round two dead trees. The steward's commands confused me and I did it wrong, which didn't help, as that confused Chita even more. I discovered later that half the others did it wrong too.

Retrieve; well, not too bad. She lost one mark on that for anticipation. She loves the exercise and flew out too soon to fetch her dumbbell, not waiting for my command. I had to wait for the steward's command, and Chita thought him far too slow.

If I make her wait, she doesn't go at all, being sure I am doing a trick stay exercise. You can't win with a dog like Chita!

Sendaway; we have practised and practised. I start her from the pole or mark on the ground from which we must send the dog, to a distance of a hundred yards or more, away from us, and walk backwards, in the opposite direction. We then turn, walk back to the mark, and I send her on.

I knew as soon as I saw the sendaway area that we were sunk. There was a fence, and the mark to send her from was only

138

two feet away from it. No way could I do her usual set up to start her. I had to sit her, which I never do. She stared at me and decided this was an Obedience sendaway as she sits at the start of that and it is very short; only a few yards. Out she went for a few yards, and then she found a scent.

She ran in circles, sniffing, oblivious to my calls of 'DOWN'. Other dogs had done the same. It was March; bucking time. The bucks had stamped in a dancing circle for half the night; the ground was full of their scent. Few dogs had ever met such a distraction. Most of us had lost before we even went on the field. There had been horses there too, another unfamiliar animal to Chita. She meets them on the roads, but we don't walk where they graze.

I can train her where sheep have been and where cattle have been; but it is difficult to find ground foiled by rabbits here, and the only time she meets deer is if the Trials is in a deer park. Dogs do need to be trained on ground that resembles that on which they will work. Those who can train their dogs while bitches are in season also have a major advantage. Few dogs work well with such a distraction, but get them used to it and you can overcome it.

I finally managed to persuade Chita to lie down. Nobody would think she could get nine out of ten for that exercise on today's showing, but it wasn't really her fault; nor mine. Circumstances were against us. Find a field with rabbits bucking and horses? Life's too short. Hope for better luck next time.

She did the agility with her usual verve and ended up with 19 out of 20. She had, as ever, been too eager to fly back over the scale. Train her better, people say. But the scale is not an exercise you can repeat over and over; it is far too much of an effort for the dog.

I had to track at eleven so decided to do the downstay at two p.m. Off in the car to the farm where Puma was bred; park where I always parked, for how many years? Was it seven? And then over to our field. One of the Manchester Police was judging and I like police judges as they always abide by the regulations and you can be sure there will be no gimmicks.

Also the track will be geared to the experience of the dog. Sometimes the lower stakes have tracks beyond the ability of the dogs taking part, as the plan of the track is too complicated.

Eric took his wife's dog recently into one stake, at my level. He said afterwards that neither Liz nor I would have managed the track which was very advanced for the dogs. He did get Sheena round, but he has been Trialling for twenty-five years. Liz and I haven't.

The field was grass; easy going. Not much wind, though still bitterly cold. Off we went like a rocket, down the side of the field, right over to the far ditch, take a right hand turn and just as I am feeling jubilant, out of the ditch came a young West Highland White dog. Over to Chita and asked her to play. I put Chita into the down position. Westie ran rings around us, barking.

He bent his legs, inviting her to get up and stop being so boring and come on, do.

The judge and steward came over, and tried to catch him. That was great fun.

By now he had thoroughly obliterated most of the second leg of the track by running across it, over and over again. She couldn't possibly carry on tracking.

Finally they made it and the judge, with a small dog tucked firmly under one arm said 'I'm sorry, you'll have to have another track. When would you like it? Twelve or four?'

Which should I choose? By four she might have switched right off. Now she was fresh. I chose to come back at twelve and went back to base for a coffee, and found lots of sympathy.

Back we went at twelve. A different field, not so good and a lot more wind.

Down the first leg, then the second leg and then the third and we came to a corner. This was beside an old dewpond, now mostly dry, but beautifully muddy in the middle with lots of animal tracks. Chita wouldn't leave it. Finally she came out, cast in a wide circle and showed me an article.

End of track.

She had found the trophy, but missed out half the track.

140

She did a beautiful search but the posts were very thin and I couldn't see the distant ones, as I need to wear glasses; but if I do wear them I need bifocals and I can't get on with those. I stepped into the square and lost Chita four marks. 56 out of 110 for the track and 31 out of 35 for the search.

Oh well, there's always next time. She jumped, startled, on the gun test; she has been a little noise-shy since the earthquake. Four out of five.

Back we went for lunch, which I ate with Ron Watkins and his wife Nell. They run the Right Way Training School at Runcorn. I went over there several Sundays for training with Chita, but it is a long way to go for half a day.

Then the downstays. Nell had done the best track of the day, but the downstay is one of her dog's problems too. We settled our dogs. Leave your dogs. We had to walk miles down the field towards the gate, out of the gate and across the yard.

It is never possible to know just what one will have to do on a stay exercise: go behind a hedge; lie down in long grass; duck into a dry ditch; go a few yards from the dog; go a few hundred yards from the dog; or leave the dog in the opposite direction to that in which it is facing.

It is a long string of hazards, compounded for Chita, I am sure, by fear of other dogs.

By the time we reached the gate, some two hundred yards from the dogs, both Nell and I had our bitches beside us.

It was worse for Nell than me, as she only needed that downstay to qualify Kay. Like me, she had been practising and practising all winter. Like Chita, her dog's stay was foolproof everywhere except in Trials on the day.

By the end of the day we had company: dogs that had failed agility; dogs that had failed control; dogs that had failed the track. Chita wasn't the lowest. She wasn't far off, but we had better marks than at least eight other dogs.

I made my way back to Macclesfield where the snow still lay thick, and consoled myself with one of Angela's lovely meals, feeling greedy, as I gave up my diet and ate what I pleased. Chita rested, quite unaware that anything at all hinges on her performance. She does her best, or what she considers her best, and she is fun to live with, so what does it matter? There's more to a dog than few pieces of paper saying it has 80 per cent.

The next day I was to collect our daughter and her new baby, Jacob, who I call Jake, who was then only nine weeks old, and bring them home for a few days. I had to pass the fields where Eric was judging and had promised to call in and see his track, which was different.

He had set up a police type incident. Each handler was given the story: there had been a break in in a chemist's shop, some of the items taken were to be found in the search square, and there was another item at the end of the track that the criminal had dropped before he was apprehended.

The dogs set off on the long tracks as this was one of the highest stakes. The article at the end of the track was a small packet of drugs. (It was actually sugar!)

In the search square were a number of other items, among them a key, part of a padlock, part of a bolt and more 'drugs'. It made it much more interesting than just the usual search for half a beer mat, a small piece of wood, a spark plug, and a wine cork, or pieces of cardboard and plastic and leather.

Chita was in the car; I had to get on.

Neither Eric nor Liz mentioned Josse.

I went back to the car. I had won a large dog bowl in a raffle the day before; something at least to show for my journey. Was it an omen? A sign saying why are you funking a new challenge? I didn't know; that seemed silly.

Another dog to learn. I envied Val her new lad. She was having fun, doing it the slow way, making sure he knew everything well before she rushed on to the next piece of teaching. So many dogs have a smattering of everything but know nothing thoroughly, which goes for us humans too, I suppose.

The groundwork is tedious. One of my club members complained that we do the same things every week, but as her dog isn't yet even beginning to understand what she wants of him, there is no choice. You can't go on to college work from the third form. The foundations must be laid.

I hadn't laid them well enough with Chita as she was so difficult at first that I missed out on the teaching years. I had to teach her not to attack every dog she met; no other training was possible except at home, where she behaved herself always.

I hadn't met Eric soon enough. Had I met him earlier it would have been quite a different story. My early instructors said that I had no future as a dog handler; I was hopeless. Eric never tells anyone that and when I asked, a little forlornly, if I was improving with Chita, he said: 'Joyce, you have improved every time I see you,' which heartens me so that I can go on trying instead of giving up.

I find that with those who come to club, it is so easy to give praise to the owners too, as most of them try very hard and I can see improvement, even if they can't.

Nothing succeeds like success, even if it's only in something small, like standing by the check-out counter at the supermarket and not being tempted into buying a bar of chocolate!

Meanwhile I had a growing temptation. It would be silly to have another dog, wouldn't it? Would it? Kenneth would say no, but then he always does. He'd said it to Janus and Puma and Chita; but I can't live without dogs.

Chita is growing older, daily.

So am I.

In another six years I probably won't have her, and then I may not feel like starting a new dog; not a German Shepherd anyway.

Josse has a good temperament; he will have his problems. There is no perfect dog.

I need more exercise.

A young dog about the place again, a dog to play with Chita. They would learn to play, wouldn't they? And this is a dog and not a bitch.

A new challenge.

A new excitement, a break from our everyday familiar rut which is so well worn that maybe both Chita and I are getting tired of it. She will need training to be with a new dog; and he will need to learn foolproof stays, and maybe if I train them together . . . .

I rang Eric.

'I will have Josse,' I said.

And that is the beginning of yet another story, still to be lived, before it is written, as Josse's coming has set me on yet another new path in life.

Chapter Fifteen

This is the fifth book about my own dogs. The first was *Two's Company*, about Janus, my Golden Retriever, and Puma, my beautiful German Shepherd bitch. The others are *Three's A Pack, Two For Joy*, and *A Dog in a Million*. These include all the dogs, and most particularly Chita, who is the only one of the three still alive. They recall the problems I had with her, as she was a horrible puppy. For two years I wondered if I could keep her; she cost me so much time and energy, and did not respond to training.

I did persist, in spite of advice to get rid of her from many experts. I am glad I did as she has taught me far more about dogs than any dog I have ever owned, and she is still teaching me. Also the books on her have helped many owners who have equally difficult dogs, as they do become biddable with time, do become far more rewarding, and life does ease. I receive so many letters from them, but my favourite begins:

'Thank you for my dog's life. If I hadn't read about your struggle with Chita I would never have tried to carry on. Now he's lovely.'

It is very easy to think that the dog you have is worse than any other, because you haven't met many dogs. It is very easy to say that it's the handler, not the dog. Certainly, the handler can't possibly teach the dog until the handler has been taught *how* to teach the dog. It doesn't come instinctively to the vast majority of us.

I always ask others to write the last words in my books on Chita. This time I have also asked people who know Chita well.

My first report comes from Barbara Swain Williams who I first met when Puma was about a year old and winning most of the classes she entered. Barbara now has three German

Shepherd stud dogs. She is a Championship judge of the breed, and writes the Welsh notes for *Dog World*.

I have known her for twelve years and she lives only a few miles away on Anglesey. She came to our dog club with Jamie, her beautiful St Bernard, who, sadly, died last year of what is thought to be salmonella poisoning. (Hugo, another St Bernard puppy has just joined the 'gang'.) Barbara also came for some months to socialise her two young dogs, Jester and Joker. We meet at shows too, so she knows Chita well. Barbara writes:

Chita today is a lovely medium-sized bitch, whose sole aim in life is to work for and please her adored owner. Her coat gleams in the sunlight, she has 'presence', she radiates health and happiness ... this is Chita now.

Such is the impression one gains on seeing Chita for the first time. But look a little closer and you will see a slight tension in the depths of those dark eyes which belies that first impression.

When I first met Chita as a baby puppy, what upset me most was that she did not want to be loved, as normal pups do, and neither could she give her love to anyone. I had not met such a pup in all my many years' association with German Shepherd Dogs.

She was a wiry, sinewy little scrap, filled with pent-up energy, emotions, inhibitions, and furies at anything or anyone that got in her way. She was a taut fiddle string, an overwound spring and a hyperactive child (all in the same body). My first reaction was 'Heaven help Joyce,' or anyone else for that matter, who had such a problem on their hands. And yet there was something there, an intangible 'something', that made me warm to her and want to reach out and help her, despite the fact that she rejected help.

In the wrong hands this pup would either have had a short unhappy life, or worse, have been passed on from home to home, each time deteriorating both mentally and physically, until she arrived at the worst sort of chained-up

146

guarding situation. In other words, a canine hell for her.

Joyce's love and unending patience have brought Chita out of her own personal anguish and transformed her into the lovely animal she now is and have earned, for Joyce, Chita's undying love and devotion. Chita would defend her to the end and ultimately lay down her own life for her.

To have known Chita is never to forget her.

Barbara has a reputation for being extremely outspoken. She is also passionate when it comes to anything that is wrong relating to dogs. Had she felt I was being a fool and making Chita out worse than she was, she would have been the first to say so.

'There's nothing wrong with the dog, it's *you*.' I've heard her say that often enough to others. Her view of Chita as being an exceptional animal helped me to persevere and gave me confidence when other people were knocking it out of me. I knew it wasn't entirely me; had I known more about dog training then I would have got on much better, but I didn't and that was that!

Chita may never win first prizes but what matters most is whether I and my dog can live happily together.

That is why I want to try and teach my owners in dog club what dogs are about and help them to enjoy their dogs as much as I do mine. It's so easy for them to complain they do the same things week after week and it's boring the dog. It isn't boring the dog; it's boring them, and they aren't trying to think of a way to liven up their training and make it more fun for both parties. The basic needs for the dog are to sit, down, stand, come, walk sensibly and not pull like a maniac, and to stay when told in the place the dog is told.

Until these are done so well we can forget they have ever had to be taught, we can't progress, as the dog isn't safe or controlled properly. Take him to an agility class and he races excitedly, totally out of control, and barks, upsetting other dogs and owners, and fights, and the class is impossible to run.

Chita could not be allowed off lead for agility work until she was five years old. Even now if other dogs are free to run and bark at her, she has to be leashed as she will retaliate and I won't have my dogs aggressive. I can't stop her always; she doesn't see why a strange dog should roar up to her and bark at her and, for that matter, neither do I. Many of my worst situations are caused by other people's thoughtlessness with *their* dogs.

One of the greatest problems many of us have here is a lady who goes regularly for walks, in the park, not only with her dog, but with her cat! The cat is well behaved and trots along beside her. She takes it out of the car, puts it under the trees, tells it to stay there, and goes back for the dog! Those of us trying to walk our own dogs are having enormous problems, as they are electrified by the sight of a ginger cat prancing along, and are dying to give chase.

The cat owner isn't very popular with dog owners and since her dog is used to the cat, is elderly and small and trots happily beside her, she hasn't the least idea of the time, energy and effort the rest of us are having in stopping our dogs from taking off after them! However, it's a free country, so I console myself with the fact that it's excellent training, even if it does nearly break my arm as I try to stop my dog flying after this tempting object. Chita doesn't do it with our cat; but that's different. I can't train her with hundreds of cats, so there will always be a new cat she hasn't been taught not to chase.

One of the people who has known Chita since her early days is Ian Westlake, who has been my accountant for fourteen years or more. He comes here four times a year, to help me with my VAT, which I find totally incomprehensible. Many of my books are published abroad so money comes in yens and dollars and marks and francs. Not a lot as the author gets paid usually about £100 for the right to translate and then comes a royalty which is often tiny. But it is all taxed in two countries so there are forms to fill in, to avoid double taxation, and if you think a tax form in English is gobbledegook try getting a Japanese or German or French tax form translated!

The UK agents take 10 per cent (VAT on that) and the overseas agent takes 10 per cent (no VAT on that) so that has to be reckoned too. Ian spends eight hours here every time he comes, battling with it. I end up convinced I am working for my agent, for my publisher, for my accountant, for the taxman; never for me!

Ian's report is brief, probably saying more in a few words than others have said in many:

'I have known Chita since she has been with Joyce. I have seen her grow from being an unusually nervous, noisy and uncontrollable young puppy into a normal friendly dog.'

Which says it all!

He was extremely tolerant as she raced at him screaming, puddled on his feet and tried to bite him. It was almost three years before she did stop puddling when she was excited or afraid and we began to think she would never get control of her bladder. She had to greet her special friends outside.

Many nervous dogs do this; people don't always realise it is nerves. If the dog is scolded, the problem simply gets worse, and the dog not only puddles in excitement or fear, but in frequent blind panic because it becomes so confused and desperate it doesn't ever gain enough confidence to sort out what the owner really means.

Don't do that doesn't mean don't do it there; to the poor bewildered dog it means, don't you ever make a puddle any-where.

Since it has natural functions that can't be denied it hangs on until it bursts; so it never gets into any sort of routine, gets more and more scolding and ends up a total nervous wreck.

I have had a number of teachers in my hunt for more knowledge. Usually, I find I come to the end of *their* know-ledge, or that in fact I know more than they do. Neither is encouraging, especially when they have set themselves up as experts.

I have gained immense knowledge on courses, but those running them always live far away and I can only spend a week with them. I need them near!

One was with Charlie Wyant, who has had four champions and trained over 100 more; another with John Seal, whose Collie, Bet, won 33 CCs. I have gained knowledge in conver-sations with Karina Smith, who won Cruft's and whose bitch is a joint Trials and Obedience Champion, which is extremely rare. There have been very few indeed.

I spent a very informative evening with John Simpson, who also won Cruft's. Cruft's is the accolade of the dog world; the show which is so hard to qualify for; you can't just enter it, you have to earn your place. Each year some fifty people out of about ten thousand work their dogs or bitches there; and two will win: one the dog class, and one the bitch class. John invited me over, when I was staying with Gina Croft near Reading. She has also won to Championship standard with her dog. At John's home I found waiting for me a number of delightful children, friends of John's own children, who had read my books and wanted autographs. His lovely German Shepherd, Courage, who was his winning dog, was alive then and lay on the carpet, a gorgeous dog, with the family rabbit between his paws.

I spent several days learning with John Cree, when I stayed in Perth. John wrote *Training the German Shepherd Dog*. He taught me how to start tracking and the sendaway; he has trained a number of Working Trial dogs, and owned the first Scottish Working Trials Champion, Quest of Ardfern.

I have spent hours picking Muriel Pearce's brains and two days on a judging course she gave to people she selected. There were six of us from a group of twenty-four. She won Cruft's four times, is one of the best judges there is, does the Cruft's commentaries and is fascinating both to watch when teaching her own dog, and to talk to.

I spent hours with the sergeant in charge of training the Cheshire dogs and I stay with the sergeant who trains the Staffordshire dogs and his wife when I go to Trials at Cannock. Endless dog talk, how they track, what they smell, what the track is like, how the wind affects it, where the scent lies, what happens on hills, in dips, where there are trees; when it is moist, or dry, or cold, or frosty, or raining in torrents.

Dog talk; the kind I only hear among genuine experts. So many people talk of other people; or of dogs in general, and don't want to find out what is really fascinating about dog

150

mentality and dog behaviour and the way a dog's mind works and the way his body works.

So that Eric Roberts is a gift from the gods.

Talk at his home is always about dogs: why does the dog do this? Was that track laid right or wrong? What did I do wrong? He trains his own dog with friends and they sit afterwards and analyse their own dog handling and each other's. That concerned and constructive analysis is something I lack, as no one here can share with me.

Sometimes I think I have found someone local but up to now it has always proved to be someone interested only in themselves and climbing on my back, and blow me. I end up teaching them for free, and miss out with Chita again.

Days at Macclesfield are days spent in Eden.

Dogs galore and all the dog talk I want.

Talking with Liz, now Eric's wife, who has also started Working Trials and was in this year's Cruft's Agility team with Sheena, her German Shepherd bitch, and with Eric about Trials; about Eric's own dog Fons, and their latest effort to win a Police Dog Stake; they have been fourth, third, second; it is never easy. It may be a bad scenting day; the dog may fail an exercise it knows well, as it isn't a robot; the handler may make a mistake, however experienced.

I began to realise I was right in thinking that Chita's failures weren't always my fault, as others said. They were sometimes due to outside conditions; a badly thought-out track; a high wind; a track that had been fouled by animals we had never seen and neither had the tracklayers; a strange place with frightening smells that panicked her. Or they were due to us having an inexperienced judge or a judge being clever and putting in a gimmick. This is very likely to throw the dog and spoil its past training.

Very old buildings often panic Chita; there is a disused wartime airfield with a ruined house that she won't go anywhere near, beside a caravan site. She trembles and pulls away.

Deer scent sends her crazy. She has only smelled it twice in her life.

151

Yes, I need to overcome it, but it's not easy to find a deer park and train daily there! The only way to cure any fault is to train over and over where the problems occur; like in a deer park, or, with a sheepchaser, beside sheepfields – not *in* them, and never when lambs are due, and always on the lead, till the dog is so used to the sight of sheep he ignores them.

And even then I would never have my dog off lead in a sheepfield.

Eric can criticise too without raising one's hackles. Yes, that's super, but don't you think it might be better to try this way? Let's see if it works for *your* dog. He has made me a far better teacher; he has made me a far more knowledgeable handler; he has made me want to try even harder; and I haven't yet even begun to exhaust his knowledge, after three years.

He praises effort, and doesn't slap his pupil down. You're hopeless!

I don't always agree with him; nor he with me, but we can differ in a civilised manner and agree to differ and remain friends. He will consider other viewpoints; really consider them, not just state forcefully: 'You're wrong. I'm the expert and I know best.' He will change his approach if something he thought would work with a dog does not work with that dog. He hasn't met that dog before. No two dogs are alike. Both of us are probably right in our own circumstances; but he is younger than I am, is male, is a professional; I am small, and I spend much of my day writing, not training dogs. It makes a difference in our approach to problems. He can use strength where I have to use cunning!

I have to use it for some of my elderly owners as there is no way they can train their dogs as they could have done twenty years ago. Eric doesn't like titbits; nor in theory do I, but there are times when I feel the titbit is the best answer to a training problem for new unskilled owners, and to make a dog that has been overtrained keen again, as overtraining does as much harm as too little training.

Chita recently has been exposed to some unskilled track-laying which demotivated her completely as the tracks were sometimes unsuitable or occasionally far too old, laid an hour or more before I came. She needs half-hour-old tracks (laid at 2 to be worked at 2.30) and until she is confident on those it is foolish to try and take her further. I was tracking with someone who had never tracked a dog, and who understands very little about Trials training of this type. So I did use a food reward at the end of the track for a time to turn her on again; difficult tracking when she is only a novice dog had made her totally uninterested in tracking, and as she had been very keen at first this was disappointing and took time to remedy.

I got over it by laying a lot of my own tracks again, and making them simple for her. It is as useless to overtax a dog and try and 'see if it can do it' as it is to offer a five-year-old who has just started to read a copy of Shakespeare's plays.

Enthusiastic newcomers often want to try out a dog and overstretch it, especially in off-lead stays; asking for far more than the dog has been taught or is capable of doing and then getting frustrated when the dog doesn't understand and gets up from a position he has just been told to hold.

Dog training has to be done stage by stage. It's no use teaching a dog to come twenty-five yards when you haven't taught him to come twenty-five inches. So many courses don't explain that the exercises shown should be taught over a long period, breaking them down into stages. They are taught in a week and those teaching assume all their hearers are much more experienced than they are and automatically know that; in fact many don't.

The good teachers do explain. Having won a number of firsts with one dog doesn't always mean that the winner can explain just how to train; or he may not even want to, as that will add to his competition!

One of my editors wrote to me to say someone writing in the same field as I am wanted to know where I get my source material. Please would I tell her? That was daft, and also a bit naughty, as if I had a store of written material I would keep it dark. It would have taken me years of research to find. In fact all my material comes from living, and I can't share that! Other

153

than in my own books. Even my fictional stories are faction; the backgrounds changed, the people invented, but the animal action is true and they are always animals I have known personally, or they don't come out true to life. I once tried to write the story of Radar, the dog in *Softly, Softly*. I only knew Radar through two short weekends, and it was a rotten book. It has never been published; I couldn't write about a dog I hadn't known well.

I could only write about Elspeth Bryce Smith in *Stranger than Fiction* because I first rode at her stables in 1962 and rode there regularly when we came to Anglesey, hearing all about her from various people. Since we moved to Anglesey in 1976, I rode with her daughter Alison several times a week for some time before she was killed by a fall from a stallion when a lorry put on its air brakes behind her on the road. It was Alison who told me how her mother rode successfully as a jockey in the 1920s, disguised as a man, and nobody found out. I can't write about real people I don't know well, and I can't write about a background I haven't shared or visited.

I found out on courses that a number of people really didn't know very much about training dogs. I had done it; they hadn't. I don't win, but that isn't what dog training is about. I train the kind of dog most people don't want to keep; and I am doing it again with Josse, who has just become part of our home.

His problem is quite unusual; but that is for another book.

The course students come home full of enthusiasm and partly digested knowledge, which they don't realise is undigested, and try to teach not only their dogs but their club dogs an exercise from the wrong end; the final stage; without ever realising time must be spent on building up to that stage and those who get to Cruft's have done just that. Months of slow very careful teaching until the dog is so confident he can obey without having to stop and think 'how do I do that?'

I watch Eric and wish I had his skill. I never will as he has worked daily with ten dogs or more, which change every three weeks, for over twelve years and before that was very involved with dog training. I can ring at ten at night in summer; Liz tells me he is out training; I can spend the day there and watch dog after dog being trained; wild dogs, good dogs, half-crazy dogs. He has endless patience, endless good humour, both with dogs and people, and a sense of humour which is vital for any teacher.

And he can criticise himself and laugh at himself, whereas others, with less knowledge, become pompous and officious and swear they know it all when they don't.

He says: 'Every single dog I meet teaches me something new, Joyce; every day of my life.'

I can appreciate that as every club dog I have also teaches me something new. They are all so different, even dogs of the same breed.

So that I value his write-up; it means a great deal to me. He writes:

Joyce is a very determined lady. Determined to further her knowledge in most aspects of animal behaviour, but especially in dog training.

In her quest for knowledge Joyce has visited a great many dog trainers up and down the country. She has travelled hundreds of miles and spent numerous nights away from home to enable her to attend as many courses on the subject as possible, amidst her very busy life as a full-time and very successful author.

Callanway Dog Training School was, I suppose, another chance to further her knowledge, or perhaps, just another waste of time.

Joyce has experienced both.

It was April 1982 when Joyce booked her first lesson. A lesson for me to assess her dog's current standard.

It was obvious that Joyce had spent a lot of time in dog training circles. She had gained knowledge; some very good, some a little questionable. She had also developed some undesirable dog handling habits – the fault of her previous instructors.

Chita was, at the time, five years old. She had been a

155

problem to Joyce right from the start, a very 'hyperactive' puppy (Joyce's terminology, not mine). All I knew was that Chita had great potential as a Trials dog. To quote a phrase we use at Callanway: 'The better the dog, the better the handler needs to be.'

The task was to improve Joyce's handling technique. As we have proved since, Chita is a dog for a very experienced handler, and not a novice handler's dog.

After the assessment we realised that we had to try to utilise the knowledge that Joyce had gained and add to it. We also realised that the biggest task was to add timing and skill to the present standard of handling.

Joyce still comes across regularly for her lessons. No mean feat when one considers the journey of 120 miles each way. It is important that she continues to improve. Not only for her own benefit but also for the sake of the dog training club which Joyce runs in Bangor.

Joyce uses much of her spare time and energy in organising and instructing at pet club level, but her greatest contribution to dog training must surely be in an advisory capacity through her books and articles.

She has helped so many people, by mail and telephone, with their doggy problems. If she hasn't the answer to a problem she isn't afraid to pick up the phone and ask advice from someone she considers may have the answer.

Having judged progress tests at her club and observed the enthusiasm and determination that Joyce puts into her dog training, and then to hear her say: 'I do my best, but I know my limitations,' I can only reply: 'Well done, Joyce, keep up the good work.'

It's so easy to rest on your laurels, to think you know it all, can do it alone, don't need to work harder, learn more.

Those in dogs who know there is so much to learn never stop learning; they go on course after course, and even at advanced levels may go to the United States or Germany to learn how

156

they do it there. More knowledge, all the time. That's what life is really about.

The last piece on Chita comes from the first man to meet her. I don't quite remember now how I got in touch with Les. I think I rang the North Wales police dog handling section in despair as here I was with what I thought was quite the most vicious thing I had ever met in puppies.

I'd met an awful lot of pups but this one was beyond my experience. She bit everything she met. She attacked everything she met, no matter if it was ten times her size.

I saw terrible trouble ahead.

I had a feeling my phone call was met with some disbelief but I had an appointment with the police dog handlers, to see if my assessment of this pup was correct.

Les Edwards is unforgettable. He is tall, with curly reddish blonde hair, with immense patience and kindness, and with immense knowledge. He also has a terrific sense of humour, and is an asset in any company.

He has helped me with tracking; he has helped me with dog club; he has boosted my morale when life kicked me in the teeth; and he has made my day by writing the piece that ends this book. He writes:

As the Police Dog Training Officer in North Wales, a position I have held since 1974, also as a Championship Obedience and Open Working Trials judge, I come into contact with many dogs, but recall clearly the afternoon I met Chita, a ten-week-old German Shepherd bitch puppy. She was confined to a purpose-built kennel in the rear of a Saab estate, accompanied by a very attractive GSD adult, and a dignified looking Goldie. The latter mentioned dogs behaved impeccably, but Chita was whining and most unsettled. I blamed the journey from Anglesey to St Asaph for this behaviour.

When removed from the vehicle and permitted to run free on a vast army camp, dear little Chita pulled aggressively on my trouser leg, much to the amusement of the other police dog handlers, enjoying a break from training. Humorous, yes, but a response that concerned me and I predicted a firm and planned training programme for this potentially difficult little madam.

Whilst acting as examiner on an advanced instructors course, with my co-examiner being none other than Muriel Pearce, we were both delighted to learn on totting up our marks that one student had gained 100 per cent in the oral test, 91 per cent in the written and equally good marks in the practical. That student was Joyce Stranger, who really impressed Muriel and me with her knowledge of dogs and their training.

Over the years Joyce has proved to me that her genuine concern to educate pet owner and instruct, help and advise at club level is most sincere and for that I applaud her.